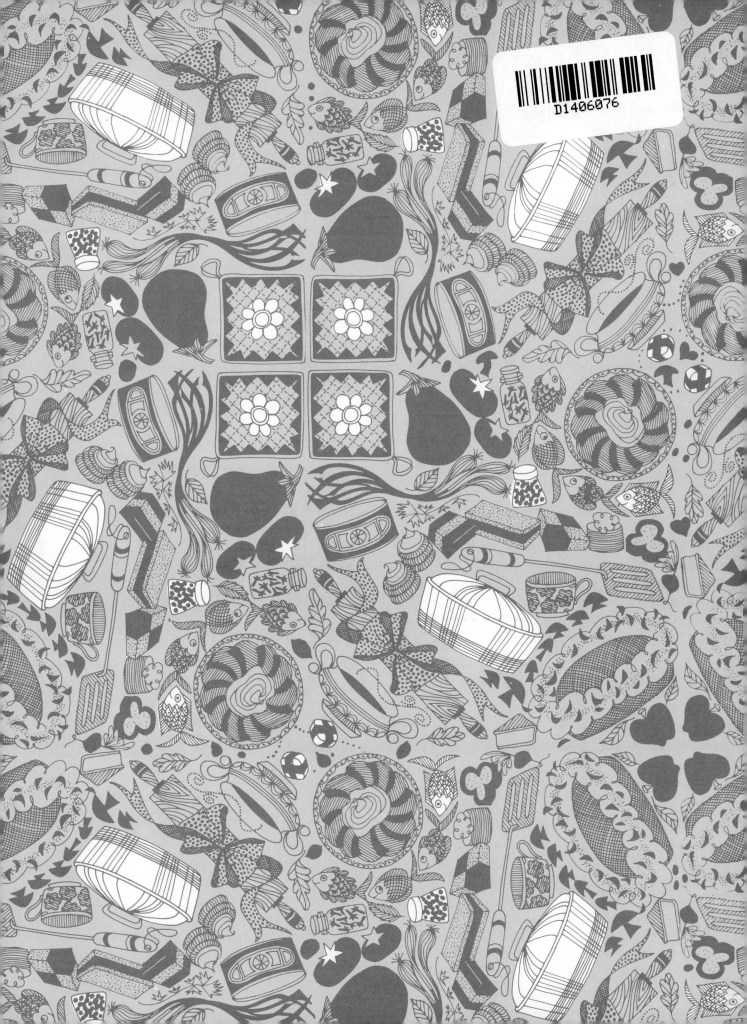

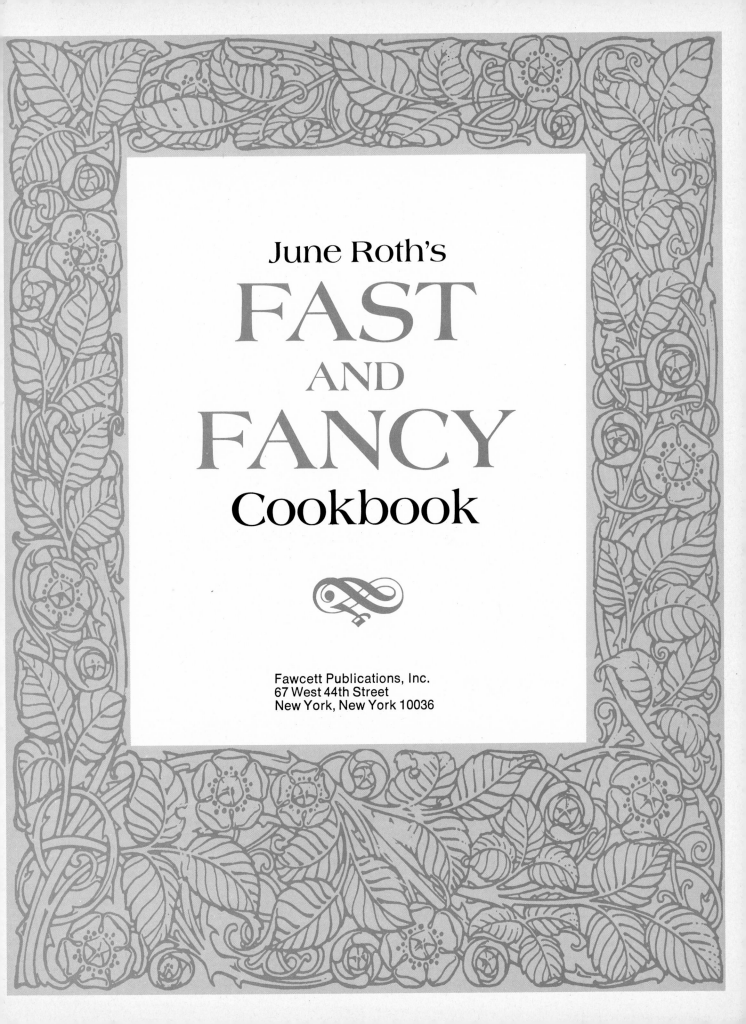

June Roth's

FAST
AND
FANCY
Cookbook

Fawcett Publications, Inc.
67 West 44th Street
New York, New York 10036

CONTENTS

Introduction 3

Weights and Measurements 4

Cooking Methods 5

Appetizers, Dips and Relishes 6

Vegetables 16

Eggs and Crepes 42

Soups 48

Seafood 52

Meat 64

Desserts 96

Index 124

LARRY EISINGER: *Editor-in-Chief*

GEORGE TILTON: *Executive Editor*

SILVIO LEMBO: *Creative Director* • HAROLD E. PRICE: *Associate Director*

ELLENE SAUNDERS: *Editor* • JOHN SELVAGGIO: *Layout*

ELAINE E. SAPOFF: *Production Editor* • ALAINE TROW: *Production Assistant*

Editorial Staff: JOE PIAZZA, RAY GILL, DAN BLUE,
FRANK BOWERS, PAMELA RIDDLE, AMY MORRIS

Art Staff: MIKE GAYNOR, ALEX SANTIAGO,
HERBERT JONAS, JOHN CERVASIO, JACK LA CERRA

Decorative Art by Ella George Calderon

Printed in U.S.A. by
FAWCETT-HAYNES PRINTING CORPORATION
Rockville, Maryland

INTRODUCTION

Look in the mirror and say hello to the lady who has a multitude of magic tricks to choose from on every shelf of her marketplace. Does m'lady realize that there are thousands of grocery manufacturers with their extensive staffs and factory workers, Madison Avenue buildings bulging with public relations promoters, and a vast army of other people connected with the food industry . . . all with one thought in mind. . . ."I wonder what she's cooking tonight!"

Do you ever feel unwanted, unloved, uncared for? Nonsense! There are people staying up nights dreaming up new convenience foods with just you in mind. Millions of dollars are spent yearly just to inform you of the products that are available to keep your family healthy, to save you time and money, to turn you into a gourmet cook at the opening of a box.

With mixer, blender, automatic can-opener, freezer, refrigerator, dishwasher, and gadgeted oven at your fingertips . . . why make the same old thing for dinner tonight? Why not take advantage of your unique position in the world, and learn to use modern products as a base for remarkable dishes that will win you applause as well as gustatorial satisfaction.

If you are a "today woman" with yesterday's tastes, blessed with an adventurous palate, you need a special kind of cookbook. So add one more person to your list of those who stay up nights dreaming of ways to make your life easier and more meaningful . . . me. Directions on boxes were designed to help you produce a good and uniform product, but everyone you know can open the same box and do the same thing. You no longer feel your offering is unique, yet you love the time and motion saved. So here is a book designed to use the boxes and the cans and combine them with imaginative tricks to turn each one into a gourmet dish.

Let the lady in the mirror reflect the smartest "cookie" you know . . . she chooses products with queenly wisdom and makes meals fit for a king!

Reflectively,

June Roth

ACKNOWLEDGEMENTS

My sincere and grateful thanks go to the following companies for their valued assistance in developing recipes and providing photographs for this book: The Aluminum Association; Arnold Bakers, Inc.; Buitoni Foods; California Raisin Advisory Board; Campbell Soup Co.; Canned Salmon Institute; Columbian Cookware; Diamond Walnut Kitchen; R. T. French Co.; General Foods Kitchens; Green Giant Co.; Hunt-Wesson Co.; Instant Potato Products Association; International Shrimp Council; Kellogg Co.; Lord-Mott Co.; Mr. Boston Distiller, Inc.; National Association of Frozen Food Packers; Nestlé; Oster Manufacturing Co.; Pineapple Growers Association; Plate, Cup and Container Institute; Processed Apples' Institute, Inc.; S. & W. Fine Foods; Sunkist Growers; Uncle Ben's, Inc.; The Underwood Kitchen; United States Brewers Assoc. Special thanks to Green Giant Co. and General Foods Inc. for providing color photographs.

WEIGHTS AND EQUIVALENT MEASURES OF COMMON FOODS

BEANS, dried navy: 1 pound=2⅓ cups uncooked=6 cups cooked

BEANS, dried kidney: 1 pound=2½ cups uncooked=6¾ cups cooked

BEANS, dried Lima: 1 pound=2½ cups uncooked=6 cups cooked

BUTTER, unwhipped: 1 pound or 4 sticks =2 cups

BUTTER, whipped: ¼ pound or 1 stick =½ cup

CHEESE, cottage: ½ pound=1 cup

CHEESE, cream: 3 ounces=6 tablespoons

CHEESE, grated: 4 ounces=1 cup

CHESTNUTS: 1½ pounds in-the-shell= 1 pound shelled

CHICKEN: 3½ pounds drawn chicken= 2 cups cooked, diced

CHOCOLATE: 1 ounce=1 square

COCOA: 1 pound=4 cups

COCONUT, finely grated: 3½ ounces= 1 cup

COFFEE: 1 pound=5 cups

CORNMEAL: 1 pound=3 cups

DATES: 1 pound=2½ cups pitted, cut

FLOUR, all-purpose: 4 ounces=1 cup sifted

FLOUR, cake: 4 ounces=1 cup plus 2 tablespoons, sifted

FLOUR, whole-wheat: 7 ounces=1 cup

MACARONI: 8 ounces=2 cups uncooked =4 to 5 cups cooked

MEAT, beef: 1 pound=3 cups cooked minced

MEAT, beef: 1 pound uncooked=2 cups ground

MUSHROOMS: ½ pound sliced raw=2½ cups

NOODLES: 2⅔ ounces=1 cup uncooked =1 cup cooked

OATS, rolled, quick-cooking: 1 pound= 5⅔ cups uncooked

OIL: 2 cups=1 pound

PEANUTS: 1 pound in-the-shell=⅔ pound of nutmeats

PEANUTS: 1 pound shelled=3¼ cups

PEAS, dry: 1 pound, cooked=2½ cups

PEAS, split: 1 pound=5½ cups cooked

PEAS, split: 1 pound, uncooked=2 cups uncooked=5 cups cooked

PECANS: 1 pound in-the-shell=½ pound nutmeats

PECANS: 1 pound shelled=4¼ cups

POTATOES: 1 pound=3 medium

POTATOES: 1 pound raw, unpeeled=2 cups cooked, mashed

RAISINS, seedless whole: 1 pound=2¾ cups

RICE: 1 pound=2½ cups uncooked=8 cups cooked

SPAGHETTI: 8 ounces=2½ cups un-cooked=4 to 5 cups cooked

SUGAR, granulated: 1 pound=2¼ cups

SUGAR, brown, firmly packed: 1 pound =2¼ cups

SUGAR, confectioners': 1 pound=3½ cups

WALNUTS: 1 pound in-the-shell=½ pound of nutmeats

WALNUTS: 1 pound shelled=4½ cups

YEAST: 1 package active dry yeast=¼ ounce or 2 teaspoons

CAN SIZES

Industry Term	Approximate Net Weight	Approximate Cups
6 ounce	6 ounces	¾
8 ounce	8 ounces	1
Picnic	10½ to 12 ounces	1¼
12 ounce	12 ounces	1½
No. 300	14 to 16 ounces	1¾
No. 303	16 to 17 ounces	2
No. 2	1 pound, 4 ounces or 1 pint, 2 fluid ounces	2½
No. 2½	1 pound, 13 ounces	3½
No. 3 cylinder	3 pounds, 3 ounces or 1 quart, 14 fluid ounces	5¾
No. 10	6½ to 7 pounds, 5 ounces	12 to 13

FROZEN FOOD PACKAGES

Vegetables	9 to 16 ounces
Fruits	10 to 16 ounces
Canned Frozen Fruits	13½ to 16 ounces
Frozen Juice Concentrates	6 and 12 ounces
Soups	10 ounces

COOKING METHODS

BAKE   To cook in the oven with dry heat.

BARBECUE   To cook over an open fire, usually outdoors.

BASTE   To moisten baking food with melted fat, gravy or wine during cooking.

BEAT   To mix ingredients briskly until smooth.

BLANCH   To immerse food quickly in boiling water, then in icy water, in order to remove fruit, vegetable, and nut skins. This technique is used to stop enzyme action before freezing fresh vegetables and fruit.

BLEND   To combine two or more ingredients with a spoon or with an electric blender, until the ingredients are indistinguishable.

BOIL   To cook in hot bubbling liquid (212°F). A rapid boil refers to vigorous bubbling, a low boil refers to gentle bubbling.

BRAISE   To brown meat in hot fat, searing all sides, then adding a small amount of liquid, covering and simmering for a long period of time.

BREAD   To dip food in crumbs until surface is covered.

BROIL   To expose food to direct heat, by cooking under or over a flame or heating element.

CARAMELIZE To cook sugar over a low heat, stirring until the sugar melts and turns light brown.

CHOP   To cut food into fine pieces.

CREAM   To mix fat and sugar together until the mixture is soft and fluffy, usually done with an electric mixer or with the back of a spoon.

CUBE   To divide into small squares.

DEVIL   To add condiments to food, making it spicy hot.

DICE   To cut food into fine cubes.

DREDGE   To coat food with flour or crumbs, until surface is completely covered.

DUST   To sprinkle food lightly with a dry ingredient, such as flour or sugar.

FILLET   To remove bones from meat or fish.

FLAKE   To break food into flat pieces, usually done with a fork.

FLAMBE   To set food ablaze.

FOLD   To mix food from the bottom of the bowl to the top, in an under-over motion that distributes ingredients without destroying air bubbles.

FRICASSEE   To stew meat in gravy, cooking it long over a low heat.

FRY   To cook in melted fat.

GLAZE   To cover food with a substance that will create a shiny finish.

GRILL   To cook by broiling on a rack.

JULIENNE   To cut food into slender strips.

KNEAD   To fold, press, and stretch dough, until it becomes smooth and elastic.

LARD   To cover lean meat or fish with strips of fat, or to insert fat into the meat with a larding needle.

MARINATE   To soak food in a mixture of oil, wine, or vinegar, and seasonings, for tenderizing and flavoring.

MINCE   To chop food very fine.

MOLD   To shape food by pouring into a desired container and then when the shape is set, removing the container.

PAN BROIL   To cook meat in an uncovered skillet, pouring off fat as it is rendered.

PARBOIL   To cook food partially in boiling water.

PAN FRY   To cook meat in an uncovered skillet, using a small amount of fat.

PARE   To cut off the peel of fruits and vegetables.

PEEL   To strip off the skin of fruit.

POACH   To simmer in hot liquid.

PUREE   To blend or force food through a strainer until it is a smooth sauce.

REDUCE   To boil a liquid down to a smaller quantity.

RENDER   To heat fat until it melts and can be poured free of connective tissue.

ROAST   To cook meat in an oven.

ROUX   A mixture formed by cooking flour and butter together, and then adding liquid to the unbrowned roux. For a brown sauce, brown the roux before adding the liquid.

SAUTE   To cook food in a small quantity of fat, usually in a skillet on top of the range, until the desired degree of brownness is attained.

SCALD   To heat liquid to just below boiling.

SCORE   To make cuts across the surface of food before roasting.

SEAR   To brown quickly, sealing in the juices, either over high heat or in a hot oven.

SIMMER   To cook in liquid, just below the boiling point, using low heat.

SKEWER   To pierce food on long pins before cooking.

SKIM   To remove floating fatty substances from liquid, usually done with a spoon.

SLIVER   To cut food into thin pieces.

STEAM   To cook food over but not touching, boiling water.

STEW   To cook food in liquid, over low heat, for a long time.

STIR   To mix ingredients with a slow circular motion.

WHIP   To beat rapidly, inflating the volume of the ingredients.

Appetizers, Dips and Relishes

Instant Hush Puppies

INSTANT HUSH PUPPIES

1 package (12 ounces) corn bread mix
1 tablespoon dehydrated minced onion
1 egg
⅓ cup beer
   Oil for frying

Combine corn bread mix, onion, egg and beer. Stir together until well blended. Drop by scant tablespoonsful into preheated hot oil (360°) and cook for 2 or 3 minutes until golden brown, turning hush puppies to brown evenly. Remove with slotted spoon and drain on absorbent paper. Repeat until all are done. Serve hot. Makes about 24.

PARTY TARTS

1 recipe pie crust mix
2 tablespoons sesame seeds
2 packages (3 ounces each) cream cheese
2 tablespoons minced chives
1 can (4½ ounces) deviled ham spread

Prepare pie crust according to directions on package, adding sesame seeds to mix. Chill and roll pastry into large rectangle, cut into about 3 dozen 2-inch scalloped rounds. Place each in a small muffin tin and bake at 400° about 15 minutes until golden brown. Cool and fill with first a layer of cream cheese mixed with minced chives, then a second layer of deviled ham. If desired, garnish with pecans, slices of radishes, olives, carrots or pimiento. Makes about 3 dozen tarts.

PARMESAN TOAST STRIPS

⅓ cup packaged corn flake crumbs
¼ cup grated Parmesan cheese
4 slices bread, toasted
⅓ cup butter
½ teaspoon onion salt

Combine crumbs with cheese. Remove crusts from toast slices, cut each slice in 5 strips. Combine butter and onion salt. Roll strips in seasoned butter, then in corn flake crumb mixture. Place on ungreased baking sheet. Bake in 400° oven for about five minutes, or until crisp. Serve at once as soup or salad accompaniment. Makes 20 strips.

HAM 'N CHEESE LOGS

24 slices cold boiled ham
1 cup dairy sour cream
½ teaspoon salt
½ teaspoon tarragon
¼ teaspoon dry mustard
24 strips Cheddar cheese, cut about ½ inch in diameter

Spread ham slices with combined sour cream, salt, tarragon and dried mustard. Top with a strip of cheese. Roll, leaving ends of cheese strips exposed. Arrange log fashion on a serving platter. Garnish with parsley. Serve chilled.

FILLED POPCORN BALLS

2 packages (8 ounces each) cream cheese
1 can (4 ounces) deviled ham
   Beer
   Buttered popcorn

Blend softened cream cheese with deviled ham. Add a few tablespoons of beer gradually until mixture is soft enough to shape into balls. Shape into 1-inch balls. Chill. Just before serving, roll balls in buttered popcorn, pressing popcorn firmly into cheese. Makes 2 dozen balls.

Parmesan Toast Strips

PIZZA TURNOVERS

- 1 **package hot roll mix or piecrust mix**
- 1 **can (8 ounces) tomato sauce**
- 1 **can (4½ ounces) deviled ham**
- ½ **teaspoon oregano**
- ½ **cup diced Mozzarella cheese**

Prepare mix according to directions on package. Roll into 18" x 12" rectangle. Cut into six 6-inch squares or twenty-four 3-inch squares. Combine remaining ingredients and spoon about 2 tablespoons of mixture on half of each square. Fold into a triangle and seal edges with a fork. Prick tops. Bake on greased cooky sheet at 425° about 15 minutes or until golden brown. Serve plain, with additional sauce or grated cheese. Makes 6 large turnovers, or 24 miniature turnovers.

SPICY HOT TWISTERS

- 1 **package refrigerated biscuits (10)**
- 1 **can (4½ ounces) deviled ham**
- ¼ **cup finely grated Cheddar cheese**

Separate biscuits and roll each biscuit into a strip about 6" x 2". Spread half of strips with a generous tablespoon of deviled ham. Cover each of the others with 2 teaspoons of grated cheese. Roll each biscuit lengthwise, seal seams and twist a ham roll with a cheese roll. Seal ends and fit into lightly oiled muffin cups. Bake at 375° for about 15 minutes, until golden brown. Makes 5 twin twists.

HOT FISH HORS D'OEUVRES

- **Peanut oil**
- 1 **jar tiny gefilte fish balls**
- ½ **cup bread crumbs**

Heat peanut oil until hot but not smoking, in a deep straight-sided pot. Drain fish balls and roll in bread crumbs. Place in a wire basket and fry until golden brown. Serve hot on toothpicks with Horseradish Dip.

HORSERADISH DIP

- ¼ **cup mayonnaise**
- ¼ **cup red horseradish**

Combine and serve in a glass bowl with the Hot Fish Hors d'Oeuvres.

SMOKED SALMON SPREAD

- ¼ **cup smoked salmon, finely chopped**
- ¼ **pound cream cheese**
- ½ **teaspoon lemon juice**
- ¼ **teaspoon prepared horseradish, white**
- 1 **tablespoon milk or cream**

Combine ingredients and chill. Serve on crackers.

Spicy Hot Twisters

STUFFED CROISSANTS

Tube of refrigerated crescent rolls
Ham Filling, or
Beef Filling, or
Shrimp Filling

Unroll dough and place triangles on lightly floured board. Fill centers of triangles. Fold as for crescents (as directed on package) or fold ends toward center overlapping each other like an envelope. Seal wide side by pinching lightly to keep filling inside. Bake on ungreased cookie sheet approximately 15 minutes or until golden brown. Serve hot or cold.

HAM FILLING

1 can (4½ ounces) deviled ham
2 tablespoons mayonnaise
  Ripe pitted olives
  Gruyere cheese (wedge), thinly sliced

Mix ham and mayonnaise to spreading consistency. Spread approximately one teaspoon on each triangle of dough. Place one or two sliced olives on ham mixture. Top with cheese. Wrap as directed above. Makes 10 Croissants.

BEEF FILLING

2 tablespoons butter
2 tablespoons onion, finely chopped
½ pound lean beef, ground
½ teaspoon chili powder
3 tablespoons tomato sauce
  Stuffed Manzanilla Olives

Sauté onion in butter until transparent. Add meat and seasonings. Cook until meat is brown. Add tomato sauce. Spread approximately 1 teaspoon on each triangle of dough. Top with sliced olives. Wrap as directed above. Makes 10 Croissants.

SHRIMP FILLING

1 can (4½ ounces) deveined small size shrimp
1 tablespoon onion, finely chopped
2 tablespoons tartar sauce
  Ripe pitted olives

Mix shrimp and onion with tartar sauce. Spread approximately 1 teaspoon on each triangle of dough. Top with sliced olives. Wrap as directed above. Makes 10 Croissants.

Flaming Walnut Pate Balls

FLAMING WALNUT PATE BALLS

1 cup butter, divided
½ teaspoon curry powder
½ cup frozen chopped onion
2 pounds chicken livers
  Seasoned salt
1 cup canned chopped walnuts
2 tablespoons chopped dried parsley
⅓ cup brandy

Heat ⅓ cup butter with curry powder in a skillet until bubbly. Add onion and chicken livers. Cook slowly until livers lose their pinkness and are done. Mash or sieve contents of skillet (or whirl smooth in blender), beating in ⅓ cup butter until entire mixture is smooth and well blended. Taste and add seasoned salt as desired. Turn into a small container, cover and chill several hours or overnight to mellow flavors and firm mixture. Shape into balls the size of a small walnut (about 36 balls), roll each one in chopped walnuts. Turn remaining ⅓ cup butter into a large skillet or shallow chafing dish. Heat until melted and bubbly. Add chicken liver balls and cook quickly a few minutes shaking pan gently to turn them. Sprinkle in parsley, add brandy and heat. Flame, shaking pan until flames die out. Serve hot with crackers or melba toast rounds. Makes 3 dozen balls.

CAMEMBERT DIP

4 ounces cream cheese, softened
2 wedges (1⅓ ounces each) Camembert cheese
3 tablespoons snipped parsley
¼ cup dairy sour cream
⅛ teaspoon black pepper

Mash first two ingredients with a fork. Stir in rest of ingredients until blended. Refrigerate until ready to use. Serve as a dip with crackers. Makes 1¼ cups.

NUTTY CHICKEN DIP

½ cup sour cream
½ cup mayonnaise
½ cup diced, cooked chicken
¼ cup chopped walnuts
2 ounces pimientos, sliced, drained
¼ teaspoon curry powder

Combine sour cream and mayonnaise. Stir in the diced chicken, walnuts, pimientos and curry powder. Refrigerate until chilled. Serve as a dip with crackers. Makes 1½ cups.

SHRIMP SOUP DIP

1 can frozen cream of shrimp soup, thawed
1 cup dairy sour cream
1 teaspoon Worcestershire sauce

Mix the thawed soup and sour cream thoroughly. Add Worcestershire sauce. Refrigerate. Serve with sturdy potato chips or crackers. Makes about 2 cups.

SOUTH OF THE BORDER DIP

1 ripe avocado, mashed
½ cup finely chopped tomato
1 tablespoon minced onion
¼ cup mayonnaise
2 teaspoons fresh lemon juice
⅛ teaspoon salt
French bread, cut in large cubes
Few drops of liquid hot pepper seasoning

Mix mashed avocado, chopped tomato, minced onion, mayonnaise, and lemon juice until well blended. Add salt and liquid hot pepper. Refrigerate until chilled. Serve as a dip with crackers. Makes 1½ cups.

AVOCADO CORN DIP

3 ripe avocados
2 tablespoons finely minced onion
2 cloves garlic, finely minced
1 tablespoon lemon juice
1 teaspoon salt
½ teaspoon chili powder
¼ teaspoon white pepper
1 can (12 ounces) whole kernel corn, drained

Peel avocados; mash with fork. Stir in remaining ingredients. Cover and refrigerate until serving time. Makes 2⅓ cups of dip.

EASY CHEESE FONDUE

Garlic
1 can condensed Cheddar cheese soup
3 tablespoons dry white wine
French bread, cut in large cubes

Rub chafing dish or top of double boiler with clove of garlic, then discard garlic. Add soup and stir until smooth. Gradually add wine. Heat, stirring now and then. To serve, spear bread cubes with fork, dunk into hot cheese.

Easy Cheese Fondue

SALMON FONDUE

- **2 tablespoons butter**
- **3 tablespoons flour**
- **1 can (7¾ ounces) salmon**
  Salmon liquid from can plus bottled clam juice to measure ½ cup
- **1 cup milk**
- **1½ cups grated Swiss cheese**
  Dash Tabasco
  French bread

In top of a double saucepan melt butter or margarine. Stir in flour. Drain salmon liquid into measuring cup and add enough clam juice until combined liquid measures ½ cup. Stir into the butter-flour mixture along with the milk and cook over simmering water until sauce is smooth and thickened, stirring constantly. Add cheese and stir until cheese is melted. Flake and add salmon. Stir in Tabasco. Cook over low heat for 5 minutes. Serve with chunks of French bread.

TWO-BEAN RELISH

1 can (16 ounces) diagonal-cut green beans,
    drained
1 can (16 ounces) diagonal-cut wax beans,
    drained
2 tablespoons diced pimiento
2 tablespoons chopped onion
⅛ teaspoon salt
¼ teaspoon garlic salt
¼ teaspoon pepper
¼ teaspoon oregano
¾ teaspoon prepared mustard
¼ cup white vinegar
¾ cup salad oil

Toss drained canned beans with pimiento and onion in large bowl. Place remaining ingredients in a small jar with tight-fitting cover. Cover and shake; pour over bean mixture. Chill 6 hours or overnight. Makes 1 quart relish.

KRAUT RELISH

1 can (1 pound) sauerkraut
½ cup sugar
½ cup finely chopped celery
½ cup finely chopped green pepper
½ cup finely chopped carrot
¼ cup finely chopped onion

Cut sauerkraut with scissors. Stir in sugar and let stand one half hour. Add remaining ingredients. Cover bowl tightly and chill at least 12 hours before serving. Makes about 8 servings.

Curry Apple Relish

CURRY APPLE RELISH

½ cup brown sugar
1 teaspoon curry powder
2½ cups canned apple slices
¾ cup seedless raisins
¼ cup apple juice
½ cup salted almonds

Combine brown sugar and curry powder; add apple slices, raisins and apple juice. Simmer about 10 minutes or until apple slices are transparent. Chill. Just before serving add almonds. Makes about 4 cups. Delicious served with pork or chicken.

SWEET & WILD RELISH

2 tablespoons butter
1 cup cashew nuts, coarsley chopped
3 tablespoons sweet pickle relish
3 tablespoons mango chutney
1 tablespoon Worcestershire sauce
    Dash of cayenne

Sauté nuts in butter until brown. Combine relish, chutney, Worcestershire sauce and cayenne with warm nuts. Serve with chops or cold leftover meat.

QUICK CORN RELISH

2 cups golden whole kernel corn (canned),
    drained
4 heaping tablespoons sweet pickle relish
3 tablespoons mayonnaise
    Prepared mustard to taste
1 tablespoon pimiento, chopped (optional)

Combine all ingredients. Serve as a relish or on a bed of lettuce as a salad.

Quick Corn Relish

CRANBERRY MINCEMEAT RELISH

1 package (9 ounces) dried mincemeat
2 cups cranberry juice cocktail
1 red apple, cored and chopped
¼ cup drained sweet pickle relish

Crumble mincemeat into a saucepan. Add cranberry juice. Bring to a boil. Simmer for 10 minutes, stirring occasionally. Remove from heat and cool. Stir in remaining ingredients. Chill until ready to serve. Makes about 3½ cups.

JIFFY RAISIN RELISH

2 cups seedless raisins
1 tablespoon instant minced onion
1 teaspoon chili powder
1 bottle (12 ounce) chili sauce
1 cup water

Combine raisins, onion and chili powder. Heat chili sauce and water to boiling, pour over raisin mixture and let stand an hour or longer. Makes about 3 cups.

y Raisin Relish

Vegetables

'TATER BEAN SALAD

- ¼ cup Italian dressing
- 1 package (16 ounces) frozen French fries
- 1¼ cups mayonnaise
- 1 teaspoon salt
- ⅛ teaspoon pepper
- 1 teaspoon prepared horseradish
- 1 teaspoon prepared mustard
- 1 can (16 ounces) diagonal-cut green beans, drained
- 4 hard-cooked eggs, sliced
- ¼ cup chopped onion

Heat Italian dressing in large frying pan; add frozen French fries. Cover and cook over low heat about 5 minutes, stirring occasionally. Blend mayonnaise with salt, pepper, horseradish and mustard. Add to French fries along with drained canned beans, eggs and onions. Toss lightly to mix and coat ingredients. Chill thoroughly. Makes about 1½ quarts salad.

FIESTA CHILI

- 1 green pepper, cut into thin strips
- ½ cup frozen chopped onion
- 2 tablespoons vegetable oil
- 2 jars (2½ ounces each) sliced mushrooms, drained
- 2 cans (15 ounces each) chili with beans
- 1 can (1 pound) tomatoes
- 1 can (8 ounces) tomato sauce
- 1 tablespoon chili powder
- 1 teaspoon oregano

In large skillet cook green pepper and onion in oil until tender. Stir in sliced mushrooms. Add remaining ingredients; cover and simmer 20 minutes. Makes 6 servings.

POLKA DOT PEPPERS

- ¾ cup frozen chopped onion
- 2 tablespoons vegetable oil
- 2 cans (8 ounces each) tomato sauce with cheese
- ½ cup snipped parsley
- 5 medium green peppers
- 1 can (15 ounces) corned beef hash
- 1 can (12 ounces) whole kernel corn, drained
- ½ teaspoon Italian herb seasoning
- ¼ teaspoon seasoned salt
- ⅛ teaspoon seasoned pepper

In saucepan sauté onion in oil until tender. Stir in tomato sauce and parsley; simmer 5 minutes. Meanwhile, cut tops from peppers; remove seeds and membrane. Cook peppers in boiling salted water for 5 minutes; drain. Combine hash, corn, Italian herb seasoning, salt, pepper and ¾ cup tomato sauce mixture; stuff peppers. Stand peppers upright in small baking dish; pour remaining sauce around peppers. Bake in preheated oven (375°) for 35 minutes. Spoon sauce over peppers before serving. Makes 5 servings.

Shown right:
Pantry Paella and Kernel Corn Bread, top
Polka Dot Peppers and Fiesta Chili, center
Calypso Kabobs, bottom

HAM 'N CHEESE LOGS

'TATER BEAN SALAD

Sweet Waikiki Beans

SWEET WAIKIKI BEANS

- 2 tablespoons shortening
- 3 tablespoons onion, chopped
- 2 No. 300 cans oven baked beans (4 cups)
- 1 cup pineapple tidbits, well drained
- 2 cups diced left-over ham
- ½ cup sliced cucumber pickles, coarsely chopped
- ¼ cup juice drained from pickles
- ¼ cup catsup
- 2 tablespoons brown sugar
- ½ teaspoon salt
  Dash Tabasco sauce

Sauté onion in shortening until transparent. Mix onion in 2-quart casserole with oven baked beans and all remaining ingredients. Bake uncovered in 400° oven for 30 minutes, or until bubbly. Serve over rice. Makes 6 to 8 servings.

GREEN BEAN CASSEROLE PARMESAN

- 1 can (1 pound) French cut green beans, well drained
- 1 can (1 pound) bean sprouts, well drained
- 1 can (5 ounces) water chestnuts, drained and sliced
- 1 can (4 ounces) sliced mushrooms, drained
- ¼ cup grated Parmesan cheese
- 3 tablespoons butter, melted
- 1 can (8 ounces) tomato sauce
- ½ teaspoon salt
- 1 can (3½ ounces) French fried onion rings

Toss vegetables with Parmesan cheese in 8- x 12-inch shallow baking dish. Sprinkle with melted butter. Combine tomato sauce and salt; pour over vegetables. Sprinkle onion rings on top. Bake in preheated oven (325°) for 20 minutes. Makes 6 servings.

Green Bean Casserole Parmesan

RICE RING

1 cup instant rice
½ cup chopped pimiento
Parsley sprigs

Cook rice according to directions on the package. Fluff up. Combine with pimiento. Pack hot rice into a ring mold. Turn out at once on hot platter. Garnish with parsley sprigs. Makes 6 servings.

ASPARAGUS SALAD ROMANA

½ cup mayonnaise
¼ cup Italian-style dressing
1 can (15 ounces) chilled, drained green asparagus spears
1 teaspoon paprika

Blend mayonnaise with dressing. Spoon over chilled asparagus spears arranged on leaf lettuce Sprinkle with paprika. Makes 4 servings.

Top left: Sloppy Josies; Center: Rice Ring, Beef Cubes Gourmet, Hunters Stew; Bottom left: Asparagus Salad Romana

NORTH STAR
BEAN BAKE

MARINATED
BEAN SALAD

TWO-BEAN RELISH

MEXICAN BEAN
CASSEROLE

BEEFED-UP BEANS

GREEN BEANS ORIENTALE

- 2 tablespoons peanut oil
- 2 packages (10 ounces each) frozen French cut green beans
- 1 small onion, cut in thin slivers
- ¼ cup soy sauce
- 1 cup slivered toasted almonds
  Black pepper

Heat peanut oil in large skillet or chafing dish add beans and slivered onions; cook 15 minutes Before removing from heat, add soy sauce, al monds and dash of pepper. Makes 6 servings

MARINATED BEAN SALAD

- 2 jars (13 ounces each) vertical-pack whole green beans
- 2 teaspoons salt
- ¼ cup sugar
- ¼ cup wine vinegar
- ½ cup salad oil
  Leaf lettuce
  Pimiento

Place drained canned beans in shallow casserole or pan. Dissolve salt and sugar in vinegar in a small jar with tight-fitting cover. Add salad oil; cover and shake. Pour over beans. Chill several hours or overnight. Serve on lettuce-lined platter garnished with pimiento. Makes 8 servings.

NORTH STAR BEAN BAKE

- 1 cup wild rice, uncooked
- 1 jar (4½ ounces) sliced mushrooms, drained
- ¼ cup butter, melted
- 2 tablespoons flour
- ½ teaspoon salt
- ⅛ teaspoon pepper
- 1 cup chicken bouillon
- 1 can (16 ounces) French-style green beans, drained
- 1 can (5 ounces) boneless chicken, drained and diced

Cook rice according to package directions. Sauté mushrooms in melted butter until lightly browned. Stir in flour and seasonings. Gradually add bouillon. Cook over low heat, stirring frequently until thickened. Add rice, drained canned beans and chicken. Place in a greased 1½-quart casserole. Bake in preheated oven (350°) for 30 minutes. Garnish with parsley and additional mushrooms, if desired. Makes 6 servings.

Chinese Bean Salad

CHINESE BEAN SALAD

- 1 can (16 ounces) diagonal-cut green beans, drained
- 1 can (16 ounces) diagonal-cut wax beans, drained
- 1 can (5 ounces) water chestnuts, drained and sliced
- ½ cup sliced red onion rings
- ⅓ cup sugar
- ⅓ cup vinegar
- 2 tablespoons salad oil
- 2 tablespoons soy sauce
- ½ teaspoon celery salt

Combine beans, water chestnuts and onion rings in large bowl. Dissolve sugar in vinegar in pint jar with tight-fitting cover. Add remaining ingredients; cover and shake. Pour over beans. Chill several hours or overnight, stirring occasionally. Makes 6 to 8 servings.

FRENCH STYLE BEAN CASSEROLE

- 1 can (15 ounces) French-style green beans
- ½ can condensed cream of celery soup, undiluted
- ½ can French fried onion rings

Drain beans and spread in shallow baking dish. Spread the soup over the beans. Crumble the onion rings and sprinkle over top. Bake in preheated oven (350°) for 20 minutes. Makes 3 servings.

BROCCOLI CHIFFON

1 package (10 ounces) young broccoli spears, frozen in butter sauce in cooking pouch
1 egg, separated
1½ teaspoons prepared mustard

Drop frozen pouch of broccoli spears in butter sauce into boiling water to cover. Bring to a second boil. Cook 16 minutes, turning several times to insure complete cooking. Do not cover pan. While broccoli is cooking, thoroughly blend egg yolk and mustard. Beat egg white until stiff peaks form. Remove pouch of broccoli from boiling water by grasping extra-long top flap. Partially open and drain butter sauce into a small saucepan. Briskly stir in mustard-egg yolk mixture. Cook over low heat, stirring constantly until slightly thickened. Fold in beaten egg white. Spoon over hot broccoli. Makes 3 servings.

CURRIED BROCCOLI SPEARS

2 packages (10 ounces each) broccoli spears frozen in butter sauce in cooking pouches
1 package (3 ounces) cream cheese
1 teaspoon instant minced onion
¼ teaspoon curry powder
1 hard-cooked egg, cut up

Slip pouches of broccoli spears into boiling water. Bring water to a second boil; continue cooking 16 minutes. Do not cover pan. Partially open pouches; drain butter sauce into saucepan. Add cream cheese, onion and curry powder. Cook over low heat, stirring constantly, until cheese is melted. Place broccoli spears on serving platter. Top with curry sauce; sprinkle with hard-cooked egg. Makes 6 servings.

SKILLET RED CABBAGE

3 tablespoons butter or bacon fat
1 small head red cabbage, shredded
1 ham knuckle, or piece of boiling beef
1 cup frozen chopped onion
1 can (1 pound) apple pie slices
½ cup red currant jelly
1 bay leaf
½ teaspoon instant seasoned meat tenderizer
¼ cup water
⅓ cup vinegar

Heat butter in skillet that has a tight-fitting lid. Add cabbage and remaining ingredients, except vinegar. Bring to a boil and reduce heat; cook at low heat about 2 hours. Add vinegar just before serving; remove bay leaf. Makes 6 servings.

CHUCK WAGON CREAMED CORN

2 thin slices of bacon
2 tablespoons onion, chopped
8 stuffed green olives, sliced
2 cups cream style canned golden sweet corn
½ cup (2 ounces) sharp Cheddar cheese, diced

Sauté bacon in skillet until crisp. Set bacon slices aside and crumble. Add onion to bacon drippings and sauté until transparent. Add sliced olives, corn and cheese. Cook over low heat until cheese melts. Sprinkle with crumbled bacon. Makes 6 servings.

For variation, beat two eggs well and blend thoroughly with corn mixture. Bake in preheated oven (350°) for approximately 35 minutes or until set. Creamed corn custard serves 6.

Chuck Wagon Creamed Corn

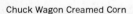

Curried Broccoli Spears

Corn Relish Salad

Corn a la Russe

CORN RELISH SALAD

1 can (12 ounces) vacuum-pack golden whole
    kernel corn, drained
¼ cup well-drained sweet pickle relish
½ cup sliced black olives
½ cup sliced celery
1 teaspoon salt
2 tablespoons sugar
2 tablespoons wine vinegar
6 tablespoons salad oil
2 quarts shredded salad greens

Combine drained canned corn, pickle relish, olives and celery. Dissolve salt and sugar in vinegar in small jar with tight-fitting cover. Add salad oil, cover and shake. Pour over corn mixture. Chill several hours, stirring occasionally. Add salad greens, tossing lightly to mix. Makes 6 servings.

CORN A LA RUSSE

6 bacon slices
¼ cup frozen chopped onion
¼ cup frozen chopped green pepper
1 tablespoon sugar
2 cups whole canned kernel corn, drained
¾ cup dairy sour cream
1 jar (2 ounces) pimientos, chopped

Sauté bacon until crisp and brown. Remove and drain on paper towel. Sauté onion and green pepper in bacon fat until onion is transparent. Add sugar and corn; heat through. Add sour cream and reheat. Garnish with bacon and pimiento. Makes 6 servings.

CORN-BRUSSELS SPROUTS DUO

1 can (1 pound, 1 ounce) whole kernel golden
   corn
½ teaspoon salt
1 package (10 ounces) frozen brussels sprouts
3 tablespoons butter
¼ cup finely chopped onion
½ teaspoon salt
⅛ teaspoon pepper

Drain corn reserving liquid. Measure ½ cup corn liquid into a saucepan and add salt. Bring to a boil, place brussels sprouts in liquid and bring to a second boil. Reduce heat, cover, and cook gently for about 8 minutes. Meanwhile, melt butter in a skillet, add onion, and sauté. Add corn, salt and pepper. Heat just to serving temperature. Place corn and brussels sprouts in a serving dish and toss lightly. Makes 6 servings.

KERNEL CORN BREAD

½ cup frozen chopped onion
2 tablespoons pure vegetable oil
1 package (14 ounces) corn muffin mix
1 can (12 ounces) whole kernel corn, drained

Cook chopped onion in oil until tender. Prepare package of corn muffin mix according to package directions. Stir in corn and cooked onion. Do not overmix. Fill generously oiled corn stick pans so batter is level with top or use a 9- x 9- x 2-inch pan. (Keep batter refrigerated until baked.) Bake in preheated oven (400°) for about 20 minutes. Makes about 21 corn sticks.

ORLEANS-STYLE CORN

1 package (10 ounces) white shoe peg corn
   frozen in butter sauce in cooking pouch
¼ cup frozen chopped green pepper
2 tablespoons frozen chopped onion
2 slices bacon, diced
1 can (8 ounces) tomatoes, undrained
1 teaspoon sugar

Slip pouch of white shoe peg corn into boiling water. Bring water to a second boil; continue cooking 12 minutes. Do not cover pan. Sauté green pepper, onion and bacon in skillet until green pepper is tender. Drain off excess fat. Stir in corn, tomatoes, and sugar; heat through. Makes 4 servings.

Orleans-Style Corn

ORANGE CORN CUPS

- 4 small navel oranges
- 1 package (10 ounces) shoe peg white corn frozen in butter sauce in cooking pouch
- 1 tablespoon frozen orange juice concentrate, thawed
- ¼ cup brown sugar
- ½ teaspoon arrowroot
- 1 teaspoon parsley flakes
- ¾ teaspoon white vinegar

Slice off about ¾-inch from stem end of each orange; remove pulp with serrated knife. Scrape out fruit with teaspoon; save for other use. Place orange cups in baking dish or in muffin tin. Slip pouch of shoe peg white corn into boiling water; bring water to a second boil; continue cooking until butter sauce is melted. Partially open pouch; drain butter sauce into small saucepan. Add orange juice concentrate, brown sugar and arrowroot; bring to boiling. Stir in parsley flakes, vinegar and corn. Spoon into orange cups. Bake in preheated oven (375°) for 25 minutes. Makes 4 servings.

EGGPLANT PARMIGIANA

- 1 medium eggplant, peeled and cut in 1-inch cubes
- ½ cup frozen chopped onion
- ½ cup frozen chopped green pepper
- ½ small clove garlic, minced
- 1 teaspoon leaf oregano, crushed
- ¼ cup butter
- 1 can (10¾ ounces) condensed tomato soup
- 1 cup water
- ¼ teaspoon salt
- 1 cup packaged croutons
- ¼ cup Parmesan cheese

Cook eggplant in boiling salted water for 3 minutes; drain and place in shallow baking dish, 10 x 6 x 2 inches. In saucepan, cook onion, green pepper, garlic, and oregano in butter until tender. Add soup, water, and salt; heat. Pour sauce over eggplant. Bake in preheated oven (350°) about 45 minutes. Remove eggplant from oven. Turn temperature up to 425°. Top eggplant with croutons; sprinkle with cheese. Return to oven and bake for an additional 15 minutes. Makes 6 servings.

CARROT-APPLESAUCE DUO

1 can (16 ounces) whole tiny carrots
1 can (16 ounces) whole sweet potatoes
1 jar (16 ounces) applesauce with apricots
1 tablespoon brown sugar
1 tablespoon grated lemon peel
2 tablespoons butter

Combine drained carrots and sweet potatoes in a shallow casserole. Mix applesauce through the vegetables. Sprinkle surface with brown sugar and lemon peel; dot with butter. Bake in preheated oven (350°) for 20 minutes. Makes 6 servings.

MINTED CARROTS-WAX BEANS

1 can (16 ounces) carrot slices
1 can (16 ounces) cut wax beans
1 tablespoon butter
1 teaspoon lemon juice
½ teaspoon chopped dried mint leaves

Empty juice from cans of carrots and wax beans into a saucepan. Heat and reduce volume of liquid to half. Add butter, lemon juice, and mint; heat until butter melts. Add carrot slices and cut wax beans; heat through. Makes 6 servings.

CAULIFLOWER WITH CHEESE SAUCE

1 large head of cauliflower
1 can cream of mushroom soup, condensed
¼ cup grated American cheese
½ teaspoon paprika

Cook cauliflower head in boiling salted water until done, but still firm enough to hold its shape. In a small saucepan, combine mushroom soup and grated cheese, heating through thoroughly. When ready to serve, pour cheese sauce over the head of cooked cauliflower and sprinkle with paprika. Makes 6 servings.

CAULIFLOWER PANE

2 packages (10 ounces each) cauliflower, frozen in cheese sauce in cooking pouches
¼ cup bread crumbs
1 tablespoon butter, melted
4 strips crisp bacon, crumbled

Slip pouches of cauliflower into boiling water. Bring water to a second boil; continue cooking 16 minutes. Do not cover pan. Stir bread crumbs into butter. Cook over medium heat, stirring occasionally, until golden brown. Open pouches; empty into serving dish. Stir in bacon. Top with bread crumbs. Makes 6 servings.

CARROT TSIMMES

1 can (16 ounces) whole tiny carrots
1 can (8 ounces) pineapple tidbits
1 cup prepared stewed prunes
1 tablespoon grated lemon rind

Empty drained can of carrots into a saucepan. Add pineapple tidbits with juice, prunes, and lemon rind. Heat through for 10 minutes. Makes 4 servings.

GOLDEN YAMS

2 cans (1 pound each) yams
6 tablespoons melted butter
¾ teaspoon grated orange rind
6 tablespoons fresh orange juice
¼ teaspoon nutmeg
¼ teaspoon cinnamon
¼ teaspoon salt
⅛ teaspoon pepper
2 tablespoons brown sugar
1 orange, sliced

Empty yams into a bowl and mash well. Beat in butter, orange rind and juice, nutmeg, cinnamon, salt and pepper. Add a little cream if the mixture seems too dry. Whip mixture until fluffy. Pile into heated serving dish; sprinkly with brown suggar and garnish with fresh orange slices. Makes 6 servings.

SCALLOPED ONIONS AND ALMONDS

    4 cups sliced, raw onions, ½" thick
   ½ cup blanched, slivered almonds
    1 can (10½ ounces) cream of mushroom soup,
        undiluted
      Salt
   ½ cup corn flake crumbs
    1 tablespoon butter, melted

Cook onion slices in boiling salted water until tender; drain. Place alternate layers of onions, almonds and soup in greased shallow 1-quart baking dish. Sprinkle each layer with salt. Combine corn flake crumbs with butter. Sprinkle over onion mixture. Bake in preheated oven (350°) about 20 minutes or until mixture is thoroughly heated and crumbs are browned. Makes 6 to 8 servings.

BROILED TOMATOES PARMESAN

    8 medium tomatoes
      Seasoned salt
      Oregano leaves, crushed
    3 tablespoons grated Parmesan cheese
    4 teaspoons butter

Wash tomatoes; cut very thin slice off blossom end of each tomato so they can be set level. Cut about ½-inch slice off stem end. Sprinkle cut tops of each tomato with seasoned salt and crushed oregano leaves. Top each with about 1 teaspoon Parmesan cheese; dot each with ½ teaspoon butter. Place on cold broiler pan and broil 5 inches from source of heat for 8 to 10 minutes, or until nicely browned and bubbly. Makes 8 servings.

SPINACH-ORANGE SALAD BOWL

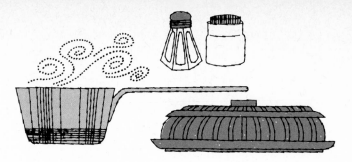

- ¼ cup lemon juice
- ½ cup orange juice
- ½ teaspoon paprika
- 1 teaspoon seasoned salt
- 1 teaspoon garlic powder
- ⅛ teaspoon black pepper
- 1 quart torn fresh spinach leaves
- 1 quart torn lettuce leaves
- ½ cup sliced radishes
- 2 oranges, peeled and cut into bite-sized pieces.

In jar, combine lemon juice, orange juice, paprika, seasoned salt, garlic powder and pepper. Cover tightly and shake thoroughly to blend. Arrange spinach leaves, lettuce, radishes, and oranges in salad bowl. Shake dressing and pour over salad. Toss lightly. Makes 6 servings.

SPINACH AU GRATIN

- 1 can (15 ounces) chopped spinach
- ½ cup grated cheese
  Salt
  Paprika
- 3 tablespoons cream

Drain spinach. Spread in shallow baking dish. Cover it with cheese, sprinkle with salt and paprika. Pour cream over cheese. Place under broiler until cheese is melted. Makes 4 servings.

Spinach-Orange Salad Bowl

SAUCY SPINACH BAKE

3 packages (10 ounces each) cut leaf spinach
   frozen in butter sauce in cooking pouches
2 tablespoons frozen chopped onion
1 package (6 ounces) whole mushrooms frozen
   in butter sauce
1 package (2¼ ounces) cheese sauce mix
¾ cup evaporated milk
2 tablespoons grated Parmesan cheese
6 strips crisp cooked bacon, crumbled
¼ cup slivered almonds

Slip pouches of spinach into boiling water. Bring water to a second boil; continue cooking 14 minutes. Do not cover pan. Partially open pouches; drain butter sauce into another saucepan. Add onion; cook until tender. Combine cheese sauce mix with evaporated milk. Add to onion. Cook, stirring constantly, until mixture just comes to a boil. Stir in Parmesan cheese. Remove frozen mushrooms from pouch. Place in medium-sized saucepan. Cook, covered, over high heat for 5 minutes. Remove cover. Reduce heat. Continue cooking, tossing lightly with fork, until butter is absorbed and mushrooms are golden brown. Add spinach, mushrooms and bacon to cheese sauce. Turn into 8 individual baking dishes or a 10- x 6-inch one. Sprinkle with almonds. Bake in preheated oven (350°) for 15 to 20 minutes. Makes 8 servings.

SPINACH WITH BACON

1 can (15 ounces) chopped spinach
2 slices bacon, chopped
¼ cup chopped cucumber or celery
4 anchovies, chopped
3 tablespoons butter
   Salt
   Paprika

Sauté bacon. Add cucumber (remove seeds) or celery. Add anchovies. Mix well. Add well-drained spinach and butter. Heat well and season with salt and pepper. Makes 4 servings.

SPINACH TIMBALES

2 cans (15 ounces each) chopped spinach
1 tablespoon butter
1 tablespoon flour
1¼ cups milk
½ cup grated Parmesan cheese
1 chicken bouillon cube
2 beaten eggs
   Salt
   Pepper

Drain spinach thoroughly. Make a white sauce of melted butter, stir in flour, then stir in milk, stirring and heating until thick. Add spinach and remaining ingredients. Butter custard cups. Fill two-thirds full of timbale mixture. Place on rack or several thicknesses of paper in a pan of hot water. Bake in preheated oven (325°) for about 25 minutes. Timbales are cooked when a knife inserted in center comes out clean. Unmold timbales and serve with creamed eggs. Makes 8 servings.

SPINACH-TOMATO RICE

1 can (1 pound, 4 ounces) tomatoes
1 package (10 ounces) frozen chopped spinach
   Dash garlic salt
   Dash instant seasoned meat tenderizer
   Pepper to taste
1 cup boiling water
1 cup minute rice

Prepare in chafing dish or covered skillet. Combine tomatoes, spinach, seasonings; bring to boil. Add water and rice; lower heat and let steam, covered, until ready to serve. Makes 6 servings.

Spinach-Grapefruit Salad

SPINACH-GRAPEFRUIT SALAD

1 can (1 pound) grapefruit sections, drained
1 tablespoon salt
1 quart fresh spinach, washed and stemmed
24 large ripe pitted olives
6 tablespoons oil
2 tablespoons vinegar

Empty grapefruit sections into bowl and sprinkle with salt. Let stand ½ hour. Tear spinach leaves into salad bowl. Place salted grapefruit sections and olives on spinach. Pour oil and vinegar over all and toss lightly. Makes 4 servings.

SPINACH WITH WHIPPED CREAM

- 1 can (15 ounces) chopped spinach
- ½ teaspoon salt
- ½ teaspoon nutmeg
- ½ cup heavy cream
- 2 teaspoons prepared horseradish
- ⅛ teaspoon mustard
- ⅛ teaspoon salt

Drain spinach and heat thoroughly. Season with salt and nutmeg. Place spinach in a baking dish. Whip cream, fold in horseradish, mustard, and salt. Heap whipped cream on spinach. Place under a hot broiler until cream is light brown. Serve immediately. Makes 4 servings.

Spinach With Whipped Cream

CREAMED SPINACH

- 1 can (15 ounces) chopped spinach
- 2 tablespoons butter
- 1½ tablespoons flour
- ¾ cup cream
- 1 tablespoon frozen chopped onion
- ½ teaspoon nutmeg
  Salt
  Pepper
- 3 anchovies, if desired

Drain spinach thoroughly. Make a white sauce by melting the butter, stirring in flour and adding the cream. When sauce is thick, add onion, spinach and seasonings. Add anchovies, mashed. Stir and cook for 3 minutes more. Serve at once. Makes 4 servings.

SPINACH RING

- 2 cans (15 ounces each) chopped spinach
- ⅓ cup butter, melted

Drain liquid from spinach, add melted butter. Press spinach into a buttered ring mold and heat in pan of water. When ready to serve, turn out on platter and fill center with buttered beets or creamed mushrooms. For a delicious luncheon or supper dish, fill center with creamed eggs, fish or chicken. Makes 6 to 8 servings.

Spinach Ring

POTATO CLOUDS

2 cups prepared instant mashed potatoes
1 cup cottage cheese
½ cup dairy sour cream
3 tablespoons frozen chopped onion
  Salt and pepper
1 teaspoon dehydrated parsley flakes
¼ teaspoon garlic salt
3 egg yolks, slightly beaten
3 egg whites, stiffly beaten

Prepare instant mashed potatoes as directed on package, omitting milk and butter. Add remaining ingredients except egg whites. Fold in beaten egg whites; pour into eight 6-ounce custard cups for individual portions, or a 2-quart casserole. Bake in preheated oven (350°) for 40 minutes. Makes 8 servings.

STUFFED BAKED POTATO

4 baking potatoes
2 tablespoons butter
2 tablespoons sour cream
¼ cup grated American cheese

Bake potatoes in preheated oven (450°) 45 minutes or until mealy. Carefully cut off tops of potatoes and scoop out into a bowl. Beat butter and sour cream into potato; spoon back into shells and top each with grated cheese. Return to oven and bake at 350° for 10 minutes, or until cheese is melted. Makes 4 servings.

SAUERKRAUT SLAW ALSATIAN

3 cups sauerkraut
2 cups frozen chopped onions
1 cup chicken consomme
1 diced green pepper
1 diced pimiento
  French dressing

In saucepan, combine sauerkraut, onions and chicken consomme. Simmer over very low heat 45 minutes. Let cool. Add green pepper and pimiento. Toss mixture with tart French dressing. Makes 6 servings.

CHEESE SWIRLED POTATOES

4 ounces Cheddar cheese
1¾ cups water
4 tablespoons butter
¾ teaspoon salt
¾ cup milk
2 cups mashed potato flakes, dried
Freeze-dried chives

Cut cheese into thin strips about 1½ inches long. Bring water, butter and salt to a boil. Remove from heat and add milk. Add potato flakes. When liquid is absorbed, stir lightly with a fork. Do not whip. Add cheese strips and stir just until cheese softens but does not melt. Spoon into serving dish and sprinkle with chives. Serve hot. Makes 6 servings.

POTATO DUMPLINGS

½ cup instant mashed potatoes
1½ cups boiling water
1 teaspoon salt
2 eggs
¼ teaspoon nutmeg
½ cup flour
Packaged croutons

Combine instant mashed potatoes, boiling water and salt. Beat in eggs, nutmeg and flour thoroughly. Mixture should be moist but not so sticky that you can't handle it with floured hands. Spoon out dough by heaping teaspoonful, place a crouton in center of each and with floured hands, shape into small ball. Drop into gently simmering salted water. Cook 10 to 12 minutes. With slotted spoon remove, draining well. Lightly toss with melted butter and sprinkle with finely chopped chives or parsley, if desired. To eat, gently pull these dumplings apart with a fork and spoon. Makes about 24 dumplings.

CHIVE RICE

1⅓ cups water
½ teaspoon salt
1⅓ cups packaged enriched pre-cooked rice
2 tablespoons chopped chives
2 tablespoons butter

Bring water and salt to a boil. Stir in rice. Cover; remove from heat. Let stand 5 minutes. Add chives and butter, mixing lightly with a fork. Makes 4 servings.

CONFETTI RICE

1 package (10 ounces) mixed vegetables frozen in butter sauce in cooking pouch
6 cups hot cooked rice
¼ cup diced toasted almonds
½ teaspoon salt
½ teaspoon fines herbs

Slip pouch of mixed vegetables into boiling water. Bring water to second boil; continue cooking 14 minutes. Do not cover pan. Combine vegetables with remaining ingredients, tossing lightly to mix. Makes 8 servings.

ZUCCHINI WITH LEMON BUTTER SAUCE

4 pounds zucchini
Water
1 tablespoon salt
4 tablespoons butter
2 tablespoons lemon juice
2 tablespoons instant minced onions
1 cup snipped parsley (optional)

Wash zucchini; slice into ⅜-inch cartwheels. Cover bottom of broad frying pan with ¾-inch cold water; add salt and bring to a boil. Add zucchini; cover and cook just until tender, but still crisp, about 8 minutes. Drain thoroughly. Melt butter in small saucepan. Add lemon juice, onions, and pour over drained squash; add parsley and toss lightly to mix thoroughly. Serve at once. Makes 8 servings.

GARDEN MEDLEY SALAD

½ fresh lime
1 avocado, peeled and sliced
1 bunch romaine lettuce
1 head iceberg lettuce
½ cup tiny cauliflower pieces
⅓ cup thinly sliced carrot
2 tomatoes, cut in wedges
1 can (10½ ounces) cut asparagus spears, chilled and drained

Squeeze lime juice on avocado slices. Line a salad bowl with romaine lettuce and avocado slices. Tear remaining romaine and iceberg lettuce into bite-size pieces. Toss with cauliflower, carrot and tomatoes, and arrange in center of salad bowl. Mound asparagus in center of bowl. Serve with Roquefort or French dressing. Makes 8 servings.

ROQUEFORT DRESSING

⅔ cup salad oil
¼ cup wine vinegar
1 medium-sized bay leaf, crumbled
¼ cup crumbled Roquefort cheese

Combine all ingredients; beat or shake until thoroughly blended. Serve over iceberg lettuce. Makes about 1¼ cups.

VEGETABLE BOUQUET SALAD

½ head cauliflour
½ head lettuce, chopped
1 can (17 ounce) sweet peas, chilled and drained
⅓ cup sliced carrots, raw
¼ cup sliced green onions
¼ cup sliced radishes

Separate cauliflower into flowerets. Place chopped lettuce in lettuce-lined salad bowl. Arrange cauliflower, peas, carrots, onions and radishes in rows on top of lettuce. Cover and refrigerate until serving time. Serve with Italian-style or Roquefort dressing. Makes 6 servings.

PEAS AUX HERBES

2 packages (10 ounces each) baby peas frozen in butter sauce in cooking pouches
1½ teaspoons dehydrated shredded green onion
1 teaspoon marjoram

Slip pouches of baby peas into boiling water. Bring water to a second boil; continue cooking 14 minutes. Do not cover pan. Open pouches of peas; empty into serving dish. Stir in onion and marjoram. Makes 6 servings.

DILLED PETITS POIS

1 package (10 ounces) baby peas frozen in butter sauce in cooking pouch
⅓ cup frozen chopped onion
2 tablespoons diced pimiento
¼ teaspoon dill weed

Slip pouch of peas into boiling water. Bring water to a second boil; continue cooking 14 minutes. Do not cover pan. Partially open pouch; drain butter sauce into small pan. Sauté onion in butter sauce until tender. Stir in pimiento, dill weed and the peas. Heat through. Makes 3 servings.

PEAS DELUXE

2 packages (10 ounces each) baby peas frozen
    in butter sauce, in cooking pouches
1 jar (4½ ounces) sliced mushrooms, drained
2 tablespoons chopped onion
¼ teaspoon nutmeg
¼ teaspoon marjoram

Slip pouches of peas into boiling water. Bring
water to a second boil; continue cooking 14 minutes. Do not cover pan. Partially open pouches of
peas; drain butter sauce into a saucepan. Sauté
mushrooms and onion in butter sauce until onion
is tender. Add peas, nutmeg and marjoram; heat
through. Makes 6 servings.

Eggs and Crepes

FLIP-TOP DEVILED EGGS

- **6 eggs, hard cooked**
- **1 can (4½ ounces) deviled ham**
- **2 teaspoons finely chopped onion**
- **1 tablespoon mayonnaise**
- **1 teaspoon lemon juice**
  Dash Worcestershire sauce

Peel eggs. Cut slice from wide end of each egg. Carefully remove yolks and mash. Mix yolks with deviled ham and remaining ingredients. Refill whites and replace "lid". Makes 6 filled eggs.

SHRIMP SAUCED OMELET

- **8 eggs, separated**
- **½ teaspoon salt**
- **4½ tablespoons butter**
- **4½ tablespoons flour**
- **1 tablespoon paprika**
- **¼ teaspoon salt**
- **1½ cups evaporated milk**
- **½ cup water**
- **1 pound frozen shrimp, cooked, cleaned and deveined**
- **1 fresh coconut, diced**

Beat egg yolks until very thick and lemon-colored. Beat egg whites until frothy; add salt. Beat egg whites until stiff; fold into yolks. Pour into two well-buttered hot 8- x 2-inch round glass baking pans. Bake in preheated oven (350°) for 15 minutes until lightly browned on top. Meanwhile, melt butter in saucepan; blend in flour, paprika and salt. Add evaporated milk and water. Cook, stirring constantly, until mixture boils and thickens. Add shrimp and coconut. Put omelets together like cake layers, spooning sauce between and over top. Makes 8 servings.

Flip-Top Deviled Eggs

Mushroom-Tuna Crepes

CREAMY SCRAMBLED EGGS WITH HERBS

- 2 tablespoons butter
- 2 frankfurters, cut into thin slices
- 6 eggs
- ½ teaspoon salt
- ¼ teaspoon pepper
- ¼ teaspoon thyme
- 1 cup dairy sour cream

Melt butter in a large skillet. Sauté frankfurters in butter until golden. Beat eggs and seasonings until well blended. Pour into skillet. Stir in sour cream. Cook over very low heat, stirring occasionally until eggs are desired firmness. Garnish with watercress, if desired. Makes 4 servings.

ARTICHOKE-PIMIENTO OMELET

- 1 jar (6½ ounces) marinated artichoke hearts
- 1 jar (3 ounces) pimiento
- 1 tablespoon butter
- 4 eggs
- ½ teaspoon salt
- ¼ teaspoon pepper
- ½ teaspoon paprika

Drain marinated artichoke hearts and add cut-up pimiento. Reserve as filling. Heat butter in a skillet. Beat eggs, add salt and pepper. Pour into skillet and cook until set. Slip omelet onto a platter, spoon artichoke-pimiento mixture over half the surface, and flip uncovered surface over filling. Makes 2 servings.

MUSHROOM-TUNA CREPES

½ cup milk
1 egg, beaten
1 tablespoon cooking oil
¼ cup flour
½ teaspoon baking powder

Combine milk, egg and oil in small bowl. Stir in flour and baking powder; blend well. Heat 8-inch skillet over medium heat; brush with oil. Pour batter, 2 tablespoonsful at a time, into skillet; tilt pan to make a 6-inch round crepe. Brown 1 minute; turn and brown other side. Stack crepes between paper toweling until ready to use. Makes 8 crepes.

FILLING

1 jar (2½ ounces) whole mushrooms, drained
1 can (7 ounces) tuna, drained and flaked
2 tablespoons diced pimiento
¼ cup mayonnaise

Combine mushrooms, tuna, pimiento and mayonnaise. Spread on crepes; roll. Place crepes seam side down in baking dish.

TOPPING

½ cup dairy sour cream
2 tablespoons light cream
⅓ cup grated Cheddar cheese

Combine sour cream and cream; spread over filled crepes. Sprinkle with cheese. Bake in preheated oven (350°) for about 15 minutes.

MUSHROOM OMELET

1 can (4 ounces) sliced mushrooms
¼ cup frozen chopped onions
1 teaspoon Worcestershire sauce
¼ teaspoon thyme
1 tablespoon butter
6 eggs
½ teaspoon salt
¼ teaspoon pepper

Empty mushrooms and juice into a small saucepan. Add chopped onions, Worcestershire sauce and thyme. Heat through. Meanwhile, melt butter in a skillet. Beat eggs, add salt and pepper, and pour into skillet. Cook until set. Slip omelet onto a platter, spoon mushroom sauce over half the surface and flip uncovered surface over filling. Makes 3 servings.

CHIVE-COTTAGE CHEESE OMELET

1 cup cottage cheese, creamed
¼ cup chopped chives
1 tablespoon butter
6 eggs
½ teaspoon salt
¼ teaspoon pepper

Mix chives into cottage cheese; reserve for omelet filling. Melt butter in a skillet. Beat eggs, salt and pepper. Pour into skillet and cook until eggs are set. Slip omelet onto a platter, spoon cottage cheese mixture over half the surface, and flip uncovered surface over filling. Makes 3 servings.

CRABMEAT OMELET

1 tablespoon olive oil
1 clove garlic, minced
1 can (7 ounces) crabmeat
1 teaspoon chopped parsley flakes
1 tablespoon butter
4 eggs
½ teaspoon salt
¼ teaspoon pepper
½ teaspoon paprika

In a small skillet, heat olive oil; add minced garlic and sauté for a minute; add crabmeat and parsley flakes, stirring until heated through. Turn off heat, and reserve for omelet filling. Melt butter in a second skillet. Beat eggs, add salt and pepper. Pour eggs into prepared skillet and cook until eggs are set. Slip omelet onto a platter, spoon crabmeat filling over half the surface and flip uncovered surface over filling. Dust surface with paprika. Serve at once. Makes 2 servings.

MINCED CLAM OMELET

1 can (10 ounces) red clam sauce
½ teaspoon oregano
1 tablespoon butter
6 eggs
½ teaspoon salt
¼ teaspoon pepper

Heat clam sauce and oregano in a small saucepan. Melt butter in a skillet. Beat eggs, add salt and pepper; pour into skillet. Cook until eggs are set. Slip omelet onto a platter, spoon red clam sauce filling over half the surface and flip uncovered surface over filling. Makes 3 servings.

BAKED BRUNCH RAMEKINS

½ pound pork sausage
1 cup cornmeal
2 teaspoons salt
½ teaspoon baking soda
1 can (8 ounces) tomato sauce with mushrooms
½ cup boiling water
3 eggs
1 cup dairy sour cream
6 eggs
1½ cups shredded Cheddar cheese

Brown sausage in a skillet; drain. Cover bottoms of six individual casseroles or ramekins with sausage. Mix together cornmeal, salt and baking soda. Pour tomato sauce and boiling water over and stir. Beat in three eggs and sour cream. Pour cornmeal mixture on top of sausage in casseroles and drop a whole egg in center of each. Sprinkle with cheese. Bake in preheated oven (350°) for 20 to 25 minutes. Makes 6 servings.

OMELET MARINARA

1 can (8 ounces) marinara sauce
¼ cup frozen chopped onion
¼ cup frozen chopped green pepper
1 tablespoon butter
6 eggs
½ teaspoon salt
¼ teaspoon pepper

In a small saucepan, combine the marinara sauce, chopped onion and pepper. Simmer for about 10 minutes. Meanwhile, melt butter in a skillet. Beat eggs, add salt and pepper; pour into skillet. Cook until eggs are set. Slip omelet onto a platter, spoon marinara filling over half the surface and flip uncovered surface over filling. Makes 3 servings.

CHERRY CREPES

1 cup sifted flour
3 eggs
1½ cups milk
½ teaspoon salt
1 tablespoon melted butter

Put all ingredients into a blender container, cover and blend until smooth. Heat a small skillet, brush with butter and pour in enough batter to cover the bottom. Tip and roll the pan if necessary in order to spread the batter thin and evenly. Brown on one side. When top is set, turn crepe. Sprinkle with confectioners' sugar and roll jelly-roll fashion. Keep warm in oven before serving. Makes 8 crepes.

CHERRY SAUCE

2½ cups canned pitted red sour cherries, not
   drained
2 whole cloves
   Piece (2″) stick cinnamon
¼ cup sugar
4 teaspoons cornstarch
½ teaspoon salt
4 teaspoons cold water
4 teaspoons corn syrup
4 teaspoons butter
2 teaspoons lemon juice
½ teaspoon red food color

Reserve 1 cup drained whole cherries. Cook remaining cherries, juice, cloves and cinnamon 5 minutes in a covered saucepan. Remove from heat and remove cloves and cinnamon. Pour cooked cherries into blender, add sugar, cornstarch, salt, water and corn syrup. Cover and blend until cherries are liquified. Pour into saucepan and bring to a rapid boil. Cook 3 minutes, stirring constantly. Remove from heat and add remaining ingredients, including the reserved whole cherries. Spoon into center of each crepe and over the rolled crepe. Serve hot.

Soups

Quick Vichyssoise

QUICK VICHYSSOISE

2 chicken bouillon cubes
½ cup boiling water
2 cans (10¼ ounces each) frozen cream of
    potato soup
2 cups milk
¼ cup chopped chives
1 cup dairy sour cream

Dissolve bouillon cubes in water. Combine bouillon, soup, milk and chives in a saucepan. Heat slowly, stirring constantly, until soup is thawed. Remove from heat and beat with a rotary beater or in a blender until smooth. Beat in sour cream. Refrigerate until well chilled, about 4 hours. Makes 6 to 8 servings.

CELERY-CABBAGE SOUP

1 can cream of celery soup
1 soup can water
¼ teaspoon caraway seed
½ cup cabbage, shredded

Stir soup to blend. Add water and caraway seed. Heat to boiling. Add cabbage. Simmer 10 minutes. Makes 3 servings.

CHICKEN SOUP AMANDINE

1 can cream of chicken soup
1 soup can milk
2 tablespoons finely chopped blanched
    almonds
1 teaspoon chopped parsley
1 drop Tabasco sauce
    Pinch of ground cloves
    Pinch of ground nutmeg

Empty soup into saucepan, stir until smooth. Blend in milk. Add remaining ingredients and heat through. Makes 3 servings.

LOBSTER BISQUE ENRICHED

2 cans lobster bisque, or cream of lobster soup
¼ cup heavy sweet cream
1 tablespoon sherry
    Additional canned lobster or shrimp
    pieces, if desired

Empty lobster soup into a saucepan. Add cream and sherry. Add additional lobster or shrimp pieces, if desired. Stir and heat through over low heat. Do not boil. Makes 3 to 4 servings.

MUSHROOM CONSOMME

1 can condensed beef bouillon
1 can water
3 large fresh mushrooms
1 teaspoon chopped parsley

Combine bouillon and water in a saucepan. Remove stems from mushrooms and reserve for later use. Wash and dry mushrooms; slice thin. Add to bouillon with parsley. Simmer for several minutes until mushrooms are cooked through. Makes 3 servings.

PUREE MONGOL

1 can cream of pea soup, condensed
1 can cream of tomato soup, condensed
1 can water
¼ cup heavy sweet cream
    Packaged croutons

In a saucepan, empty the pea and tomato soups. Add a soup can of water and the sweet cream. Blend thoroughly and heat over low flame for several minutes until hot. Serve with croutons floating. Makes 4 servings.

PEA SOUP PROVENCAL

1 can clear chicken broth, condensed
1 can green split pea soup, condensed
1½ soup cans water
1 teaspoon Worcestershire sauce
¾ cup fine noodles, uncooked

Combine soups, water and Worcestershire sauce. Bring to a boil, add noodles. Cover tightly, reduce heat and simmer 10 minutes or until noodles are tender. Makes 4 servings.

SALMON-MUSHROOM SOUP

1 can cream of mushroom soup, condensed
1 cup milk
1 can (7¾ ounces) salmon, including liquid
¼ teaspoon ground pepper
½ teaspoon paprika
¼ cup cooking sherry
1 teaspoon lemon juice

Combine soup, milk, and salmon liquid. Flake and add salmon. Stir in remaining ingredients. Heat over simmering water or stir over direct heat. Makes 3 servings.

BROCCOLI SUPREME SOUP

1 package (10 ounces) broccoli spears frozen
  in butter sauce in cooking pouch
1 can (10½ ounces) condensed cream of
  chicken soup
1 cup light cream
¼ teaspoon beau monde seasoning
  Dairy sour cream
  Watercress

Slip pouch of broccoli spears into boiling water.
Bring water to a second boil; continue cooking
16 minutes. Do not cover pan. Open pouch;
slip contents into blender; whirl until smooth.
Add soup, cream and beau monde seasoning;
blend thoroughly. Chill at least 4 hours. Serve
with a dollop of sour cream and garnish with a
sprig of watercress. Makes 4 servings.

JELLIED TOMATO CONSOMME PARISIENNE

3 cans (12 ounces each) tomato juice, divided
1½ envelopes unflavored gelatin
3 tablespoons lemon juice
  Salt to taste
3 teaspoons minced parsley
6 slices lemon
  Dash of cayenne (optional)

Soften gelatin in ¾ cup tomato juice. In saucepan, heat remaining tomato juice to boiling;
add to gelatin and stir until thoroughly dissolved.
Add all remaining ingredients except lemon
slices and cayenne. Pour into small loaf pan;
chill until firm. To serve, cut into cubes with
knife, garnish with lemon slices and dash of
cayenne. Makes 6 servings.

Broccoli Supreme Soup

RED HOT TUREEN

2 cans (10¾ ounces each) condensed tomato
    soup
½ cup apple juice
2 cups water
    Dash ground cloves
    Dash cinnamon
    Dairy sour cream

Blend tomato soup with remaining ingredients
except sour cream. Heat; stir now and then. Garnish with sour cream. Makes 6 servings.

TOMATO CORN SOUP

1 can tomato soup
1 soup can water
2 whole tomatoes, cut in thin wedges
½ cup whole kernel corn, drained
2 tablespoons onion, minced
1 teaspoon parsley, chopped
½ teaspoon Worcestershire sauce

Combine soup and water, stir until smooth. Add
remaining ingredients. Heat to boiling and simmer five minutes until onion and tomato are tender and flavors are blended. Makes 3 servings.

TOMATO NOODLE SOUP

1 can cream of tomato soup, condensed
1 can chicken noodle soup, condensed
1 can milk
1 teaspoon chopped parsley

In a saucepan, combine tomato and chicken
noodle soups. Add 1 soup can of milk. Heat and
blend over low flame. Serve with a sprinkling of
parsley. Makes 4 servings.

TOMATO SOUP SMETENA

1 can tomato soup, condensed
½ soup can milk
½ cup sour cream
    Chopped chives

Blend soup and milk thoroughly. Chill and serve
with a dollop of sour cream, sprinkled with
chopped chives. Or blend all together and serve
hot. Makes 3 servings.

CURRIED SALMON AND PEA SOUP

2 tablespoons butter
1 tablespoon minced onion
1 teaspoon curry
1 can pea soup, condensed
1 can (7¾ ounces) salmon, flaked
    Liquid from salmon plus milk to measure
        1½ cups
1 teaspoon lemon juice

In a saucepan, heat butter and in it cook onion
and curry until onion is soft. Stir in remaining
ingredients. Heat and stir until heated through.
Makes 3 servings.

SALMON CHOWDER

1 can cream of celery soup, condensed
1 can (7¾ ounces) salmon, flaked
    Liquid from salmon plus milk to measure
        1½ cups
½ teaspoon paprika
1 tablespoon chopped parsley
½ teaspoon dried dill weed

Blend celery soup in a saucepan. Add flaked
salmon, salmon liquid and milk. Add paprika,
parsley and dill. Heat over simmering water or
stir over direct heat. Makes 3 servings.

Salmon Chowder

Seafood

CREAMED SHRIMP AND EGGS

⅓ cup butter
⅓ cup flour
2 cups milk
1 teaspoon salt
¼ teaspoon pepper
2 teaspoons grated horseradish
4 hard-cooked eggs, coarsely chopped
2 cups frozen shrimp, cooked and cleaned
2 tablespoons chopped parsley
2 cups corn flake crumbs
2 tablespoons melted butter

Melt butter; stir in flour. Add milk slowly, stirring constantly. Cook until thickened, stirring occasionally. Stir in salt, pepper and horseradish. Chop shrimp coarsely. Fold in eggs, shrimp and parsley. Spread in greased 10- x 6-inch baking pan or shallow casserole. Combine corn flake crumbs with melted butter. Sprinkle over shrimp mixture. Bake in preheated oven (350°) about 25 minutes or until thoroughly heated. Serve at once. Makes 6 servings.

SHRIMP-RICE BAKE

¾ cup shortening
1 cup frozen chopped onion
4 cups canned tomatoes
1 teaspoon Worcestershire sauce
½ teaspoon paprika
¼ teaspoon hot pepper.
⅛ teaspoon mace
2 teaspoons salt
2 pounds frozen shrimp, shelled and deveined
4 cups cooked rice
6 strips bacon

In skillet, melt shortening. Add onion, tomatoes, Worcestershire sauce and seasonings. Cook over low heat, stirring occasionally for about 20 minutes. Add shrimp and cook 10 minutes more. If desired, prepare early and refrigerate until ready to bake. Add rice. Turn into a greased 3-quart casserole. Arrange bacon strips over rice mixture. Bake in preheated oven (375°) for about 25 minutes. Makes about 8 servings.

FRENCH-FRIED SHRIMP WITH TOMATO-WINE SAUCE

1½ cups chili sauce
½ cup tomato juice
½ teaspoon Worcestershire sauce
    Dash Tabasco
½ teaspoon chili powder
1 clove garlic
¼ cup dry wine
1 tablespoon lemon juice
1 bay leaf
1 clove
2 packages (10 ounces each) frozen breaded shrimp

Combine sauce ingredients in a jar. Cover and let stand several hours. Strain and serve with French-fried shrimp, prepared according to package directions. Makes 6 to 8 servings.

SEAFOOD EN COQUILLE

1 package (10 ounces) peas frozen in butter sauce in cooking pouch
2 tablespoons flour
1 cup milk
1 cup grated Cheddar cheese
3 tablespoons cooking sherry (optional)
⅛ teaspoon white pepper
2 cans (6½ ounces each) crabmeat, drained and flaked
1 can (4½ ounces) large shrimps, drained
2 tablespoons butter, melted
⅓ cup fine bread crumbs
    Paprika

Slip pouch of peas into boiling water. Bring water to a second boil; continue cooking until butter sauce is melted. Open pouch; drain butter sauce into medium saucepan. Stir in flour; gradually add milk. Place over medium heat; cook until thickened, stirring constantly. Add cheese; heat until melted. Stir in sherry, pepper, crabmeat and shrimps. Spoon into four large greased baking shells; allow ¾ cup per serving. Combine butter and bread crumbs. Sprinkle around outside edge of baking shells. Bake in preheated oven (350°) for 25 minutes. Dust with paprika. Makes 4 servings.

Shrimp Rice Bake

Seafood En Coquille

SHRIMP ESPANOLA

2 pounds shrimp, shelled and deveined
1 cup olive oil
½ cup lemon juice
2 tablespoons minced fresh parsley
   Pinch powdered saffron (optional)
1 tablespoon grated onion
½ teaspoon salt

In refrigerator, marinate the shrimp in mixture made from combining remaining ingredients; leave in marinade for 24 hours, stirring occasionally. Remove from marinade, grill under broiler just until bright pink, about 5 minutes. Serve hot with the marinade as a sauce. Serve with rice pilaf, made by adding golden raisins to rice while it is boiling. Makes 6 servings.

Ratatouille Shrimp Casserole

BREADED SHRIMP WITH SOUR CREAM SAUCE

  2 packages (1 pound each) frozen breaded
     shrimp
  1 cup dairy sour cream
½ cup chili sauce
  1 teaspoon Worcestershire sauce
  1 teaspoon prepared horseradish
  1 teaspoon grated onion
½ teaspoon salt
½ teaspoon celery salt

Prepare frozen breaded shrimp according to directions on package. Combine remaining ingredients for sauce. Makes 6 servings.

TUNA-WILD RICE BAKE

  1 box (6 ounces) Long Grain and Wild Rice
  3 tablespoons finely chopped onion
¼ cup butter
⅓ cup flour
  1 teaspoon salt
¼ teaspoon pepper
  2 cups milk
  2 cans (7 ounces each) tuna fish
¼ cup chopped ripe olives
  1 tablespoon lemon juice
⅓ cup mayonnaise
⅓ cup crushed potato chips
  2 diced, hard-cooked eggs

Cook rice according to package directions. Sauté onions in butter. Add flour, salt and pepper and blend. Stirring vigorously, add milk gradually. Cook until thickened. Add rice, tuna fish, olives, lemon juice, mayonnaise and 3 tablespoons potato chips to the sauce and mix well. Fold in diced eggs. Pour into a baking pan and cover with the remaining potato chips. Bake in preheated oven (425°) for 30 to 40 minutes. Makes 6 to 8 servings.

SHRIMP LASAGNA

- 2 packages (10 ounces each) frozen peeled and deveined shrimp
- 1 can (8 ounces) tomato sauce
- ¼ teaspoon oregano
- ¼ teaspoon garlic powder
- ¼ cup water
- 1 can (2 pounds, 8 ounces) lasagna
- 8 ounces ricotta cheese
- 8 ounces Mozzarella cheese, sliced thin
- 3 tablespoons grated Parmesan cheese

Thaw shrimp. Combine tomato sauce, oregano, garlic powder and water in a saucepan. Bring to a boil. Add shrimp and bring back to boil, then simmer two minutes. Grease a 2-quart casserole. Line the bottom with half the lasagna. Top with half the shrimp, using a slotted spoon to lift them from the sauce. Scatter half the ricotta and the Mozzarella over this. Repeat all the layers. Then add enough tomato sauce mixture so it becomes visible around edges of noodles and cheese. Sprinkle surface with Parmesan cheese. If desired, prepare early and refrigerate until ready to bake. Bake in preheated oven (375°) for 30 minutes, or until mixture is bubbling and beginning to brown. Remove from oven and let stand five minutes to firm. Makes 6 servings.

Shrimp Lasagna

RATATOUILLE SHRIMP CASSEROLE

- 1 medium eggplant, peeled and sliced ¼-inch thick
- 1½ tablespoons lemon juice
- ½ cup olive oil, divided
- 4 medium cloves of garlic, crushed
- 2 cups frozen chopped onion
- 1 tablespoon salt
- ½ teaspoon freshly ground pepper
- 2 cups frozen chopped green pepper
- 5 small zucchini, sliced thin
- 5 large tomatoes, sliced thin
- 2 pounds frozen shrimp, cleaned but not cooked

Peel and slice eggplant. Sprinkle lemon juice over sliced eggplant. In a 4-quart Dutch oven, heat ¼ cup olive oil; sauté half the crushed garlic for 1 minute, then sauté half the onion for 1 minute more, without browning. Combine salt and pepper; sprinkle a little over the onion. Arrange half the vegetables and shrimp in layers, sprinkling each layer with salt and pepper: peppers, eggplant, zucchini, tomatoes and shrimp; sprinkle with half the remaining garlic and a little olive oil. Repeat the layers, beginning with onion and finishing with tomatoes and shrimp. Sprinkle with last bits of garlic and remaining oil. Bring to a boil; reduce the heat to a fast simmer; cover, and cook twenty minutes. Remove cover and continue cooking to reduce sauce, about another ten minutes. Sauce may be thickened further by stirring in a blend of two teaspoons soft butter and two teaspoons flour. Makes 6 servings.

QUICK SPAGHETTI CLAM SAUCE

- 1 pound spaghetti
- 1 can red clam sauce
- ½ teaspoon oregano
- ¼ teaspoon garlic powder

Cook spaghetti in boiling water as directed on the box. In a small saucepan, empty red clam sauce and stir in oregano and garlic powder. Cover and simmer until the spaghetti is cooked and drained. Serve spaghetti at once with hot clam sauce. Makes 3 to 4 servings.

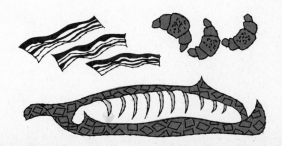

SALMON RING WITH BRUSSELS SPROUTS

1-pound can salmon with liquid
2 tablespoons butter
½ cup frozen chopped onion
¼ cup frozen chopped green pepper
1½ cups soft bread crumbs
Grated rind of 1 lemon
1 tablespoon lemon juice
¼ teaspoon hot pepper sauce
2 eggs, slightly beaten

Flake salmon into a bowl and add liquid from can. Melt butter and in it sauté onion and pepper for about 5 minutes, or until onion is transparent. Add to salmon along with remaining ingredients. Mix well and pack mixture into a well-greased 4-cup ring mold. Set mold into pan containing 1 inch hot water and bake in a preheated 350° oven for 30 minutes. Turn out and fill center with creamed sprouts.

CREAMED BRUSSELS SPROUTS

2 packages (10 ounces each) frozen brussels sprouts
3 tablespoons butter
¼ cup frozen chopped onion
3 tablespoons flour
1 cup chicken broth
Salt and pepper to taste
⅛ teaspoon nutmeg
¼ cup cream
2 tablespoons minced parsley

Cook sprouts, covered, in boiling salted water for 10 minutes, or until just tender. Drain. Meanwhile, in top of double saucepan, melt butter over direct low heat. Add onion and sauté for about 5 minutes or until transparent. Stir in flour. Remove from heat and stir in chicken broth. Return to heat and cook, stirring constantly, until sauce is smooth and thickened. Add salt and pepper to taste. Stir in nutmeg, cream, parsley, and sprouts. Keep hot over simmering water. Serve in center of Salmon Ring.

WINE BROILED SALMON

3 1-inch thick salmon steaks, fresh or frozen
2 tablespoons melted butter
¼ cup white wine
1 teaspoon dill

Arrange salmon steaks on a broiling pan. Melt butter in a saucepan; add wine and dill. Pour over salmon steaks. Broil steaks for 15 minutes, or until flaky. Makes 6 servings.

3 tablespoons butter
½ cup frozen chopped onion
3 tablespoons flour
½ cup milk
1 teaspoon salt
⅛ teaspoon pepper
2 egg yolks
1-pound can salmon, drained and flaked
1 cup fresh bread crumbs
Flour
1 egg, beaten with 2 tablespoons water
Fine dry bread crumbs
Hot deep fat for frying

In a saucepan melt butter and sauté onion in it for 5 minutes. Stir in flour. Gradually stir in milk and cook over low heat until thickened, stirring constantly. Remove from heat and beat in salt, pepper, and egg yolks. Stir in salmon and fresh bread crumbs. Refrigerate 30 minutes or until ready to use. Shape mixture into 2-inch nuggets. Roll in flour, dip in egg mixture, and coat with dry crumbs. Fry in hot deep fat (375°) for 4 to 5 minutes, or until golden brown. Drain on absorbent paper, pile while piping hot on serving dish, and serve with favorite cream sauce or with Smetane Sauce. Makes 4 servings.

SMETANE SAUCE

2 tablespoons butter
2 scallions or green onions, chopped
¼ teaspoon salt
Dash pepper
½ cup chicken stock or white wine
1 cup dairy sour cream

In a skillet melt butter. Add scallions and sauté for 5 minutes. Add salt, pepper, and stock or wine; boil until liquid is reduced to about half. Stir in sour cream and simmer until sauce is thickened. Strain into gravy bowl.

Shown right:
Veal and Succotash en Casserole
Kernel Corn Bread
Dilled Petits Pois
Wine Broiled Salmon

Macaroni-Salmon Rarebit Casserole

MACARONI-SALMON RAREBIT CASSEROLE

    2 boxes (8 ounces each) packaged macaroni
         and cheese dinners
    1 can or bottle (12 ounces) beer
 3½ cups water
         1-pound can salmon, drained and flaked
    ¼ cup chopped stuffed olives
    ¼ cup finely chopped celery
    1 can (3½ ounces) French fried onions

Prepare macaroni and cheese according to package directions for oven method by placing macaroni in ovenproof casserole; sprinkle cheese mix on top. Heat beer and water together to boiling point; pour over macaroni and cheese. Cover and bake in a preheated oven (375°) for 20 minutes. Remove casserole, mix in salmon, olives and celery. Stir all together, cover, and return to oven for 10 minutes more. Remove again and place a layer of French fried onions over top. Bake for another 5 minutes, uncovered, just until onions are heated and crisp. Makes 6 to 8 servings.

DANISH SALMON CASSEROLE

    8 ounces dehydrated sliced potatoes, cooked
         1-pound can salmon
    2 cans cream of celery soup
    1 cup milk
    3 tablespoons dehydrated onion flakes
    ¼ cup dehydrated parsley flakes
    4 tablespoons chopped pimiento
    2 tablespoons lemon juice
    1 teaspoon dry mustard
    1 teaspoon dill weed
    ¼ teaspoon pepper
    2 slices buttered toast, quartered
    ⅓ cup grated Cheddar cheese

While potatoes are cooking, drain and flake salmon into a saucepan. Add soup, milk, onion and seasonings and heat over low heat, stirring occasionally. Drain potatoes and arrange alternate layers of potatoes and the salmon mixture in a buttered 2-quart casserole, ending with salmon mixture. Garnish with bread triangles sprinkled with cheese. Bake in preheated oven (350°) for 30 minutes. Makes 6 servings.

SALMON RABBIT

3 tablespoons butter
1 small onion, minced
½ green pepper, minced
2 tablespoons flour
1-pound can salmon
Liquid from can of salmon plus bottled clam juice to measure 1 cup
Dash Tabasco
1 cup grated Cheddar cheese
¼ teaspoon salt, or to taste
¼ cup cream

In a saucepan melt butter. Add onion and green pepper and sauté for 10 minutes, or until onion is golden. Stir in flour. Drain liquid from can of salmon into measuring cup and add clam juice to make 1 cup. Stir into flour mixture and cook over low heat, stirring until sauce is smooth and thickened. Flake and add salmon. Stir in Tabasco, cheese, salt, and cream and continue to cook, stirring, until cheese is melted. Serve over hot buttered toast. Makes 4 servings.

CURRIED QUICHE

½ pound frozen Alaska King crab
1 tablespoon lemon juice
2 tablespoons cooking sherry
1 tablespoon finely chopped onion
1 teaspoon parsley flakes
¼ teaspoon curry powder
1 package (9 ounces) frozen French fried potatoes
2 tablespoons butter
1 frozen 10-inch pastry shell
1 cup shredded Swiss cheese
1 jar (5 ounces) sliced mushrooms, drained
3 eggs, well beaten
¾ cup evaporated milk
1 teaspoon salt

Drain crab meat and slice, reserving 3 large pieces cut in half for garnish. Combine sliced crab, lemon juice, sherry, onion, parsley flakes and curry powder. Refrigerate for 2 hours to blend flavors. Cut potatoes, reserving 6 long strips, into ½-inch pieces. Sauté pieces in butter until golden brown. Cover bottom of pastry shell with Swiss cheese. Spread crab meat mixture and potato pieces over cheese. Top with mushrooms. Combine eggs, evaporated milk and salt. Pour into pastry shell over all. Garnish with reserved crab meat and potato strips. Bake in preheated oven (350°) for 45 minutes or until custard is lightly browned and set. Cool slightly and cut into wedges. Makes 6 servings.

BROCCOLI-CRAB DIVAN

2 packages (10 ounces each) young broccoli spears frozen in butter sauce in cooking pouches
¼ cup onion, chopped
1 package (1 pound) frozen Alaska King crab
1 can (10½ ounces) condensed cream of mushroom soup
¾ cup shredded Cheddar cheese

Slip pouches of broccoli into boiling water. Bring water to a second boil; continue cooking for 15 minutes. Partially open pouches; drain butter sauce into saucepan. Add onion; sauté until tender and butter sauce is almost absorbed. Place broccoli spears in shallow casserole. Arrange crab meat, drained and sliced, over broccoli. Combine onions, mushroom soup and cheese. Pour over crab and broccoli, allowing some of the broccoli to show around the edges. Bake in preheated oven (350°) for 15 to 20 minutes until heated and slightly brown on top. Makes 6 servings.

FLORENTINE CASSEROLE

1 package (10 ounces) cut leaf spinach, frozen in butter sauce in cooking pouch
½ pound frozen Alaska King crab
1 cup shredded Cheddar cheese, divided
1 can (8 ounces) tomato sauce
1 cup dairy sour cream
2 tablespoons flour
1 teaspoon instant minced onion
⅛ teaspoon nutmeg
1 package (1 pound) frozen French fried potatoes
Parsley flakes

Slip pouch of cut leaf spinach into boiling water. Bring water to a second boil, continue cooking 10 minutes. Combine spinach, drained and sliced crab meat, ½ cup cheese, tomato sauce, sour cream, flour, instant minced onions and nutmeg. Turn into a 1½-quart casserole. Sprinkle with remaining cheese. Bake in preheated oven (350°) for about 30 minutes. Meanwhile, prepare French fried potatoes according to package directions. Sprinkle with parsley flakes. Serve with casserole. Makes 4 to 6 servings.

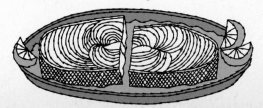

HAWAIIAN FILLETS

    4 fish fillets, fresh or frozen
    2 tablespoons butter
    2 tablespoons flour
    ½ cup evaporated milk
    ½ cup water
    ¼ teaspoon salt
    ⅓ cup mayonnaise
    1 teaspoon instant onion
    1 tablespoon prepared mustard
    1 teaspoon sugar
    1 tablespoon chopped pickles or green olives
    1 tablespoon chopped parsley
    1 tablespoon capers
    4 fresh pineapple spears
    8 large onion rings
       Melted butter
    4 frozen fried fish portions

Thaw frozen fillets. Melt butter in saucepan; blend in flour. Add evaporated milk and water; cook, stirring constantly, until mixture boils and thickens. Add salt, mayonnaise, instant onion, prepared mustard, sugar, chopped pickles, parsley and capers; blend well. Spread each fish fillet with 1 tablespoon sauce; arrange pineapple spears and onion rings on each fillet and roll up. Secure with toothpick. Place fillets in buttered baking dish and brush with butter. Arrange fish portions on baking sheet. Bake both in preheated oven (350°) for 25 minutes; arrange fish fillets and fish portions alternately on a platter over Confetti Rice (see Index). Makes 8 servings.

Also shown: Confetti Rice, Garden Medley Salad

LOBSTER-WALNUT SALAD CANTONESE

1 tablespoon butter
1 tablespoon soy sauce
1 cup walnuts, large pieces and halves
1 cup diagonally sliced celery
½ cup sliced green onions
1 can (5 ounces) water chestnuts, drained and sliced
1 can (11 ounces) Mandarin orange segments, drained
3 cups cooked lobster chunks
Sweet-Sour Dressing (recipe follows)
Salad greens

Melt butter, add soy sauce and walnuts. Stir gently over low heat until walnuts are lightly toasted, about 10 minutes. Remove and cool. Combine well chilled celery, onion, water chestnuts, orange segments and lobster. Add just enough Sweet-Sour Dressing to hold ingredients together. Fold in walnuts. Pile on crisp salad greens. Serve with additional dressing if desired. Makes 6 servings.

SWEET-SOUR DRESSING

3 eggs
½ cup granulated sugar
2 tablespoons all-purpose flour
2 teaspoons seasoned salt
⅛ teaspoon curry powder
⅓ cup strained lemon juice
⅓ cup cider vinegar
1 can (14½ ounces) evaporated milk
1 tablespoon soft or melted butter

Beat eggs. Beat in sugar, flour, salt and curry powder. Blend in lemon juice and vinegar. Cook in top of double boiler over boiling water until mixture thickens, about 10 minutes. Stir frequently to keep smooth. Beat in undiluted evaporated milk and butter. Cool, then store in covered container in refrigerator. Makes about 3 cups dressing.

Lobster-Walnut Salad Cantonese

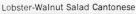

CRAB A LA PARMENTIERE

1 package (1 pound) frozen potato rounds
1 package (10 ounces) peas frozen in butter sauce in cooking pouch
1 package (6 ounces) whole mushrooms frozen in butter sauce in cooking pouch
2 tablespoons flour
1½ cups milk
½ cup shredded Cheddar cheese
1 tablespoon instant minced onion
¾ teaspoon seafood seasoning
2 cans (7½ ounces each) Alaska King crab
1 tablespoon cooking sherry

Spread potato rounds in single layer on a shallow baking pan. Bake in preheated oven (425°) for about 15 minutes. Meanwhile, slip pouch of peas into boiling water. Bring water to a second boil, continue cooking 14 minutes. Also, remove frozen mushrooms from pouch and place in another saucepan. Cover and place over medium heat for 7 minutes. Remove cover and continue cooking for several minutes, tossing lightly with a fork until butter sauce is absorbed and mushrooms are golden brown. Partially open pouch of peas. Drain butter sauce into mushrooms. Add flour. Gradually stir in milk. Add cheese, instant onion and seafood seasoning. Cook over medium heat, stirring until mixture is thick. Add crab, drained and flaked, peas and sherry. Heat through. Serve topped with potato rounds. Makes 6 servings.

BAKED SEAFOOD SALAD

2 cups corn flakes
2 tablespoons butter, melted
1 cup cooked crabmeat
1 cup cooked, cleaned shrimp
½ cup frozen chopped green pepper
¼ cup frozen chopped onions
1 cup finely cut celery
1 cup mayonnaise
½ teaspoon salt
1 teaspoon Worcestershire sauce
Paprika

Crush corn flakes slightly; combine with melted butter. Reserve this for topping. Flake crabmeat, removing bones and membranes. Combine crabmeat, shrimp, green pepper, onions, celery, mayonnaise, salt and Worcestershire sauce; mix lightly. Spread in individual shells or in a 9- x 9-inch shallow baking pan. Sprinkle with corn flake mixture and paprika. Bake in preheated oven (350°) for about 30 minutes. Serve with lemon slices, if desired. Makes 6 servings.

Baked Seafood Salad, Crab a la Parmentiere, Broccoli-Crab Divan, and Curried Quiche

Meat

SURPRISE MEATBALLS

- 1½ pounds lean ground beef
- 1 cup fine dry bread crumbs
- 2 tablespoons finely-chopped onion
- 2 eggs, beaten
- ¼ cup milk
- 1 teaspoon salt
- ⅛ teaspoon pepper
- 6 ounces blue cheese, cut into small chunks
- 2 tablespoons shortening, melted
- 1 can (10½ ounces) mushroom steak sauce

Lightly but thoroughly combine meat with bread crumbs, onion, eggs, milk and seasonings. Shape into 1½-inch balls around chunks of blue cheese (be certain that all cheese is sealed in). Brown in small amount of melted shortening in large heavy frying pan. Stir in mushroom steak sauce; cover and simmer about 20 minutes. Makes about 18 meat balls.

QUICK SPAGHETTI MEAT SAUCE

- 1 pound thin spaghetti
- ½ pound lean chopped beef
- 2 tablespoons olive oil
- ¼ cup dried onion flakes
- ¼ cup dried parsley flakes
- 1 can (15 ounces) tomato sauce
- ½ teaspoon basil
- 1 teaspoon oregano

Cook spaghetti in boiling water as directed on the box. Meanwhile, in a large skillet, brown the chopped beef in 2 tablespoons olive oil, breaking up the meat into small particles as it browns. Add onion flakes, parsley flakes and tomato sauce. Stir well. Add basil and oregano. Cover and simmer until spaghetti is done. Drain spaghetti and serve with hot meat sauce. Makes 3 to 4 servings.

SWEDISH MEATBALLS

- 1 cup prepared instant mashed potatoes
- 1 pound ground beef
- ½ pound ground pork
- 1 egg
- 2 tablespoons dehydrated onion flakes
- 1 teaspoon sugar
- 1 teaspoon salt
- ¼ teaspoon pepper
- ¼ teaspoon nutmeg
- ⅛ teaspoon allspice
- ⅛ teaspoon ginger
- 2 tablespoons butter

Prepare one cup instant mashed potatoes as directed on package. Combine all ingredients except butter; mix thoroughly. Form into tiny balls, using about 1 level tablespoon of mixture per ball. Melt 2 tablespoons of butter in a skillet; add meat balls, browning them over low heat and shaking pan occasionally to brown evenly. Makes 48 meatballs.

Pictured at left: Surprise Meatballs

Swedish Meatballs

SPAGHETTI WITH MEATBALLS

- 1 pound lean ground beef
- ¼ cup fine dry bread crumbs
- 1 teaspoon salt
- ¼ teaspoon pepper
- ¼ cup milk
- ¾ cup frozen chopped onion, divided
- 1 clove garlic, minced
- 2 tablespoons cooking oil
- 2 cans (8 ounces each) tomato sauce
- ½ cup water
- 1 teaspoon Worcestershire sauce
- 1 teaspoon basil, crumbled
- ½ teaspoon oregano, crumbled
- ½ pound spaghetti, cooked

Combine meat, bread crumbs, salt, pepper, milk and ¼ cup onion. Form into 18 meat balls. Brown in oil. Remove meatballs and sauté remaining onion and garlic. Add tomato sauce, water and seasonings. Stir in meatballs and simmer 30 minutes. Cook spaghetti according to package directions. Drain and serve hot with sauce and meat balls. Makes 6 servings.

BEEF SCALLOPINE WITH MUSHROOM SAUCE

2½ **pounds top round beef, sliced ¼-inch thick**
Instant seasoned meat tenderizer
2 **tablespoons salad oil**
1 **cup frozen chopped onion**
1 **clove garlic, minced**
1 **can (4 ounces) mushrooms**
1 **teaspoon pepper**
1 **cup dry red wine**

Thoroughly moisten meat with water. Sprinkle tenderizer evenly, like salt, over entire surface of pieces of meat. Pierce with fork at ½-inch intervals. Sauté onion and garlic in salad oil, in a skillet. When lightly browned, add mushrooms, pepper and wine. Simmer for 10 minutes. Remove from skillet, add more oil and sauté beef slices about 1 minute on each side for rare. Return mushroom mixture to skillet; heat through with meat; serve at once. Makes 6 servings.

STEAK DIANE

3 **pounds round steak, cut into individual**
steaks ¼-inch thick
¼ **cup butter, divided**
½ **cup frozen chopped onion**
½ **cup snipped parsley**
1½ **tablespoons chili sauce**
1 **teaspoon prepared mustard**
Freshly ground pepper
3 **tablespoons lemon juice**
1 **tablespoon Worcestershire sauce**
¼ **cup cognac**

Moisten the surface of the meat with water, sprinkle meat tenderizer evenly, like salt, over the entire surface. Pierce at ½-inch intervals. Refrigerate meat until ready to cook. In a skillet or chafing dish, heat 1 tablespoon butter. Sauté steaks individually until just brown; transfer to hot platter. Add remaining butter to pan; add onions and cook 1 minute only, to tenderize them. Combine seasonings and add; blend and heat through. Return steaks to skillet, coating each steak with sauce; then transfer back to platter. Pour remaining sauce over steak. Pour cognac into skillet to absorb remaining sauce, then pour over steaks and set aflame. Serve at once. Makes 6 servings.

BEEF STROGANOFF

2 **pounds lean chuck or round beef**
Instant seasoned meat tenderizer
3 **tablespoons shortening, divided**
1 **cup frozen chopped onion**
1 **cup sliced mushrooms, canned or fresh**
2 **tablespoons flour**
2 **cups beef bouillon or consomme**
3 **tablespoons sherry wine**
3 **tablespoons tomato paste**
1 **teaspoon dry mustard**
⅔ **cup dairy sour cream**

Moisten meat with water, sprinkle meat tenderizer evenly, like salt, over entire surface of the meat. Pierce with fork at ½-inch intervals over surface of meat. Cut into strips 2½" long x ¾" wide x ½" thick, removing all fat and gristle. In a skillet, melt 2 tablespoons of the shortening; sauté mushrooms and onion about 15 minutes, until lightly browned. Remove to dish. Add remaining tablespoon of shortening to skillet; sear beef strips quickly on both sides, about 2 minutes. Beef must be rare. Remove meat to dish with mushrooms. Add flour to skillet, brown well. Add bouillon slowly, stirring constantly, to make a smooth sauce. Add sherry, tomato paste and mustard; blend well. Add meat, mushrooms and onions. Simmer about 15 minutes; about 5 minutes before serving, add sour cream, blending well into sauce. Makes 6 servings.

TERIYAKI

2 **pounds top round beef, cut very thin**
(⅛ inch)
Instant meat tenderizer
2 **teaspoons ground ginger**
2 **cloves garlic, minced**
2 **tablespoons sugar**
¼ **cup soy sauce**
½ **cup water**

Moisten all surfaces of the meat and sprinkle instant tenderizer evenly, like salt, over the entire surface. Pierce at ½-inch intervals. Combine ginger, garlic, sugar, soy sauce, and water to make sauce. Place meat in bowl and pour sauce over. Marinate in refrigerator for several hours before cooking time. Remove meat from marinade, pan-broil in chafing dish or electric skillet to desired degree of doneness, about 6 minutes total cooking time for rare. Makes 6 servings.

SKILLET BEEF SUPREME

1½ pounds top round steak
2 tablespoons flour
1 teaspoon salt
⅛ teaspoon pepper
2 tablespoons butter
1 cup sliced onions
⅓ cup beef bouillon
1 can (15½ ounces) spaghetti sauce with mushrooms
½ cup dairy sour cream

Cut the meat into strips, 3- x ½-inch. Mix flour, salt and pepper. Coat meat with seasoned flour. In a large skillet melt 2 tablespoons butter and cook onions until tender but not brown. Add meat and brown lightly. Add bouillon and spaghetti sauce. Cover and cook over low heat for 25 minutes. Remove cover. Stir in sour cream. Do not let mixture boil. Serve with cooked noodles or rice. Makes 4 to 6 servings.

LONDON BROIL FLAMBE

3 pounds flank steak
Instant seasoned meat tenderizer
1 can (3 ounces) broiled sliced mushrooms
1 can beef gravy
¼ cup cognac, warmed

Moisten meat with water, sprinkle meat tenderizer evenly, like salt, over entire surface of the meat. Pierce with fork at ½-inch intervals over surface of meat. Broil steak about 4 minutes on each side. Meanwhile, combine mushrooms and gravy and heat. Pour mushrooms and gravy over steak on platter, pour cognac over steak and set aflame. Serve at once, slicing steak diagonally, across the grain, in thin slices. Makes 6 servings.

SHORT RIBS OONA LOA

6 to 8 pounds lean beef short ribs
Instant seasoned meat tenderizer
1⅓ cups pineapple syrup from canned slices
½ cup soy sauce
½ cup honey
1 cup water
2 tablespoons brown sugar
1 large clove garlic, pressed
2 teaspoons ground ginger
8 pineapple slices (canned)

Moisten the surface of the meat and sprinkle tenderizer evenly, like salt, over the entire surface of the meat. Pierce deeply every ½-inch. Place ribs in bowl. Combine all remaining ingredients except pineapple slices and pour over ribs. Cover loosely with waxed paper; refrigerate 4 hours, or overnight. Half an hour before serving time, remove the ribs from the sauce; place on barbecue grill set 4 inches from hot coals. Cook until well browned, about 20 minutes, turning frequently and basting with sauce during grilling. About 10 minutes before ribs are done, dip pineapple slices into sauce; place on grill with ribs and brown quickly on both sides. Makes 6 servings.

Skillet Beef Supreme

STEAK AU POIVRE

3 pounds round steak, cut 1½-inches thick
Instant meat tenderizer
¼ cup whole peppercorns, cracked
2 tablespoons butter
¼ cup cognac

Moisten meat with water, sprinkle meat tenderizer evenly, like salt, over entire surface of the meat. Pierce with fork at ½-inch intervals over surface of meat. Press pepper into both sides of steak with heel of hand. Heat butter in skillet until it smokes; add steak and brown quickly on both sides. Cook to desired degree of doneness, about 12 minutes for rare. Transfer steak to hot platter. Add cognac to pan; swirl it around and pour over steak. Serve at once. Makes 6 servings.

SAUERBRATEN POT ROAST

4 pounds beef brisket, or bottom round
1 package instant meat marinade
⅔ cup white vinegar
4 whole cloves
4 peppercorns
1 bay leaf
1 onion, sliced
1 carrot, sliced crosswise
1 rib celery, sliced
2 tablespoons oil or shortening
2 tablespoons flour
⅓ cup finely crushed gingersnaps

Pour contents of package of instant meat marinade into a Dutch oven or heavy skillet with tight-fitting lid. Thoroughly blend in vinegar; add cloves, peppercorns, bay leaf, onion, carrot and celery. Place meat in marinade. Pierce all surfaces of meat thoroughly with fork. Marinate 15 minutes, turning several times. Cover tightly and simmer over low heat until meat is nearly tender, about 1½ hours; remove meat. Pass vegetables and gravy through sieve; measure the puree and if necessary, add water to make 2½ cups. Set aside. Melt oil in Dutch oven; blend in flour and brown to a rich golden color; stir in puree mixture. Add meat, cover and continue cooking over low heat until meat is tender, about ½ hour. Or cook covered in preheated oven (325°) about ½ hour. Remove meat to warmed serving platter. Add crushed gingersnaps to pot juices; blend well. Cook until thickened. Serve over meat. Makes 6 to 8 servings.

MUSTARD STEAK SAUCE

3 egg yolks
⅓ cup prepared yellow mustard
6 tablespoons butter, at room temperature
½ teaspoon seasoning salt
Dash cayenne pepper

In a saucepan beat the egg yolks with a rotary beater until thick and lemon-colored. Add mustard; blend well. Warm mixture over very low heat, or in top of double boiler, stirring constantly. When mixture begins to thicken, add butter in three portions, beating well after each addition with rotary beater. Blend in salt and cayenne. Keep warm, uncovered, over hot water. (If sauce begins to separate, add a teaspoon of cold water, and beat with a fork until smooth.) Serve warm sauce spooned over steak.

SLOPPY JOSIES

1 pound lean ground beef
2 tablespoons melted shortening
1 teaspoon seasoned salt
⅛ teaspoon seasoned pepper
1 tablespoon instant minced onion
1 teaspoon Worcestershire sauce
1 can (5¾ ounces) mushroom steak sauce
6 hamburger buns, sliced and toasted

Brown meat in a small amount of melted shortening in heavy frying pan. Stir in seasonings and mushroom steak sauce. Heat thoroughly. Spoon into hamburger buns. Makes 6 servings.

CORN MEDLEY CASSEROLE

½ cup uncooked elbow macaroni
1 pound ground beef
¾ teaspoon salt
⅛ teaspoon pepper
½ cup frozen chopped green pepper
½ cup frozen chopped onion
1 can (12 ounces) whole kernel corn, drained
1 can (10¾ ounces) condensed tomato soup
1 can (8 ounces) tomato sauce with cheese
5 drops hot pepper sauce
3 slices American cheese, cut in
    half diagonally

Cook macaroni according to package directions; drain. Brown ground beef in large skillet. Add salt, pepper, green pepper and onions; brown until onions are tender. Stir in cooked macaroni, corn, soup, tomato sauce and pepper sauce. Turn into a 1½-quart casserole. Top with cheese slices. Bake in preheated oven (350°) for 30 minutes. Makes 6 servings.

BROILED ROUND STEAK

2½ pounds top round steak, cut 1½ inches thick
    Instant meat tenderizer
    Black pepper
2 packages (6 ounces each) whole mushrooms frozen in butter sauce in cooking pouches
2 tablespoons Burgundy wine

Moisten one side of the steak; sprinkle with meat tenderizer and pierce with fork over entire surface. Repeat process on other side. Broil meat about 3 inches from heat for about 8 minutes. Season with pepper and turn to other side. Broil until well browned and cooked to desired doneness (about 8 minutes on second side for medium rare). Meanwhile, remove frozen mushrooms from pouches. Place in large saucepan. Cover; place over high heat for 5 minutes. Remove cover; reduce heat; continue cooking tossing lightly with a fork until butter is almost absorbed. Add burgundy wine and continue cooking until wine has evaporated and mushrooms are golden brown. Serve over steak cut in thin diagonal slices. Makes 6 servings.

BEEF CUBES GOURMET

1½ pounds beef cubes
2 tablespoons melted shortening
½ teaspoon salt
⅛ teaspoon pepper
½ cup water
1 can (10½ ounces) mushroom steak sauce
1 can (17 ounces) small early peas, drained
¼ cup sour cream

Brown meat in a small amount of melted shortening in large heavy frying pan. Add seasonings and water; cover and simmer until meat is tender, about 40 minutes. Add more water if necessary to prevent meat from becoming dry. Stir in mushroom steak sauce and drained canned peas. Heat thoroughly. Remove from heat and stir in sour cream. Serve over hot buttered rice or noodles. Makes 6 servings.

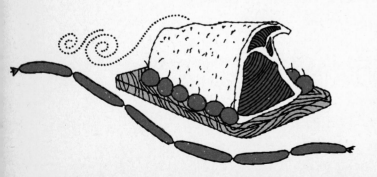

MEXICAN BEAN CASSEROLE

1 pound lean ground beef
1 egg, slightly beaten
¼ cup chopped onion
¾ teaspoon salt
2 tablespoons melted shortening
2 tablespoons flour
2 cans (8 ounces each) tomato sauce
½ cup chopped green pepper
½ teaspoon salt
1 teaspoon chili powder
¼ teaspoon cumin powder
⅛ teaspoon cinnamon
3 cans (16 ounces each) French-style wax beans, drained
    Processed American cheese slices, cut in triangles

Lightly but thoroughly combine meat with beaten egg, onion and ¾ teaspoon salt. Shape into small balls. Brown in melted shortening in a large skillet. Drain off excess fat. Sprinkle flour over meat, stirring lightly. Add remaining ingredients, except beans and cheese. Simmer several minutes or until slightly thickened. Stir in drained canned beans. Spoon into greased 2-quart casserole. Bake in preheated oven (400°) about 30 minutes. Several minutes before end of baking time, top with cheese triangles. Makes 8 servings.

SAUCE-TOPPED MEAT LOAF

1½ pounds lean ground beef
½ cup fresh bread crumbs
2 eggs
½ cup chopped onion
1 teaspoon salt
¼ teaspoon pepper
2 cans (8 ounces each) tomato sauce with tomato bits

Combine beef, bread crumbs, eggs, onion, salt and pepper with ⅓ cup tomato sauce. Shape into loaf in shallow baking pan. Bake in preheated oven (350°) for 1 hour; pour off excess fat. Pour remaining tomato sauce over loaf. Bake 10 minutes longer. Makes 6 servings.

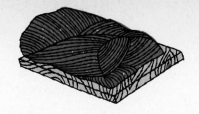

BEEF BOURGUIGNON A LA MARINADE

4 to 5 pounds stewing beef, cut into 2-inch cubes
1 package instant meat marinade
⅔ cup Burgundy wine
1 cup frozen chopped onion
3 carrots, cut diagonally in 1-inch pieces

Pour contents of package of instant meat marinade into large shallow pan. Add wine; blend thoroughly. Arrange meat in marinade mixture in a single layer. Pierce all surfaces of meat thoroughly with fork. Marinate 15 minutes, turning several times. Place meat and marinade mixture in a large skillet or Dutch oven with tight-fitting lid. Add onion; cook over low heat, turning each piece of meat once. When liquid begins to bubble, reduce heat and simmer, covered, 1 hour. Add carrots; simmer tightly covered 1¼ hours more, or until carrots are tender. Makes 8 servings.

CASSEROLE CON QUESO

1 pound ground beef
½ cup frozen chopped onion
Shortening
8 5-inch tortillas, cut into strips
1 can (12 ounces) whole kernel corn with sweet peppers, drained
1½ cups chili sauce
½ teaspoon salt
½ teaspoon cumin powder
1½ cups grated Cheddar cheese

Brown beef and onion in small amount of melted shortening in a large skillet. Sauté cut tortillas until all the pieces are coated and are crisp. Drain. Combine all ingredients except half of cheese. Spoon into greased 1½-quart casserole; top with remaining cheese. Bake in preheated oven (350°) for 30 minutes. Makes 6 servings.

Skillet Chops and Rice, Chicken Marengo, and Sauce-Topped Meat Loaf

CASSEROLE JARDINIERE

2 packages (10 ounces each) mixed vegetables frozen in butter sauce in cooking pouches
1½ cups uncooked medium egg noodles
¼ cup frozen chopped onion
1 can (8 ounces) tomato sauce
½ cup dairy sour cream
½ pound wieners, cut in ½-inch pieces
½ cup shredded Cheddar cheese

Slip pouches of mixed vegetables into boiling water. Bring water to a second boil; continue cooking 14 minutes. Do not cover pan. Cook noodles in boiling salted water according to package directions. Drain. Partially open pouches of mixed vegetables; drain butter sauce into saucepan. Sauté onion in butter sauce until tender. Combine noodles, mixed vegetables, onion and remaining ingredients except cheese. Turn into a 1½-quart casserole. Sprinkle with cheese. Bake in preheated oven (350°) for 25 to 30 minutes. Makes 6 servings.

CALYPSO KABOBS

8 ounces elbow macaroni, cooked and drained
1 can (16 ounces) diagonal-cut green beans, drained
2 cans (8 ounces each) tomato sauce
½ teaspoon seasoned salt
1 can (12 ounces) luncheon meat, cut in 12 chunks
1 green pepper, parboiled and cut in 12 pieces
6 canned peach halves, cut in half
½ cup frozen chopped onion
1 small clove garlic, minced
2 tablespoons vegetable oil
1 teaspoon Worcestershire sauce

Combine macaroni, green beans, 1 can tomato sauce and seasoned salt; place in shallow baking dish. Alternate chunks of luncheon meat, green pepper pieces and peach quarters onto skewers; arrange on top of macaroni mixture. Cook onion and garlic in oil until golden. Add Worcestershire sauce and remaining can tomato sauce; spoon over kabobs. Bake in preheated oven (375°) for 20 to 25 minutes or until heated through. Makes 4 servings.

Casserole Jardinere

HUNTERS' STEW

2 cans (10½ ounces each) mushroom steak
    sauce
1 can (12 ounces) beef loaf, cubed
1 can (17 ounces) peas with onions, drained
1 can (16 ounces) small whole potatoes,
    drained
1 can (8 ounces) diced carrots, drained

Heat mushroom steak sauce in medium saucepan. Add cubed meat and drained canned vegetables. Heat thoroughly, stirring occasionally.
Makes 6 to 8 servings.

SKILLET SUPPER

8 wieners
½ cup sliced celery
¼ cup butter, melted
¼ cup flour
½ teaspoon salt
2 cups milk
1 teaspoon grated onions
½ cup shredded American cheese
1 (16-ounce) can diagonal-cut green beans,
    drained
2 cups diced cooked potatoes

Cut wieners in short, thin strips. If desired, reserve one wiener, cut in long strips, to garnish
casserole. Sauté wieners and celery in butter in
large frying pan; remove. Stir flour and salt into
remaining butter. Gradually blend in milk. Cook
over low heat, stirring constantly, until thickened
and smooth. Add meat, celery and remaining ingredients. Cover; cook over low heat about 10
minutes, stirring occasionally. Makes 6 servings.

BAKED BEAN CASSEROLE

2 cans (1 pound each) pork and beans
    with tomato sauce
2 tablespoons brown sugar
¼ teaspoon dry mustard
⅛ teaspoon cinnamon
1 tablespoon instant minced onion
1 cup dairy sour cream
12 slices Canadian-type bacon
6 frankfurters, sliced crosswise

In a 1½-quart casserole combine beans, brown
sugar, dry mustard, cinnamon, onion and sour
cream. Arrange bacon slices and frankfurters
on top of beans. Push into beans to partially
cover meat. Bake in a preheated oven (325°)
for 45 minutes. Makes 6 servings.

PANTRY PAELLA

1 cup raw rice
½ cup frozen chopped onion
½ cup frozen chopped green pepper
2 tablespoons vegetable oil
1 can (12 ounces) corned beef, cut in chunks
1 can (4 ounces) Vienna sausages,
    cut in chunks
1 can (8 ounces) tomato sauce
1½ cups water
1 can (8½ ounces) peas, drained
½ cup sliced ripe olives

In skillet brown rice, onion and green pepper
in oil. Add corned beef, Vienna sausage chunks,
tomato sauce and water; cover and simmer 20
minutes. Stir in peas and olives. Cover and
continue cooking 10 minutes or until rice is done.
Makes 6 servings.

BEEFED-UP BEANS

2 cans (12 ounces each) corned beef
¼ cup diced green pepper
¼ cup butter, melted
1 cup dairy sour cream
½ teaspoon dill seed
¼ teaspoon salt
⅛ teaspoon pepper
2 cans (16 ounces each) whole wax beans,
    undrained

Break up corned beef, using a fork. Sauté with
green pepper in melted butter until lightly
browned. Stir in sour cream blended with dill
seed, salt and pepper. Heat thoroughly over
very low heat; do not boil. While meat sauce
is cooking, heat and drain canned beans. Serve
topped with hot sauce. Makes 8 servings.

CREAMED CHIPPED BEEF

1 jar (3½ ounces) chipped beef, cut
¼ cup butter
¼ cup unsifted all-purpose flour
2½ cups milk
¼ cup thinly sliced ripe olives
¼ cup thin strips pimiento
¾ teaspoon Worcestershire sauce
    Dash of pepper

If chipped beef seems too salty, rinse in hot
water before using. Sauté chipped beef in butter until lightly browned. Add flour, stirring
until blended. Gradually add milk, stirring constantly. Cook and stir over medium heat until
sauce is smooth and thickened. Add olives,
pimiento, Worcestershire sauce, and pepper.
Garnish with hard-cooked egg wedges, pimiento
and black olives, if desired. Makes 4 servings.

Saucy Beans and Franks

VEAL AND SUCCOTASH EN CASSEROLE

1½   **pounds veal round steak**
  3   **tablespoons butter, melted**
  1   **jar (2½ ounces) sliced mushrooms, drained**
⅓   **cup sliced green onions**
  2   **cups undiluted canned chicken broth**
¼   **teaspoon celery salt**
⅛   **teaspoon pepper**
  5   **tablespoons flour**
⅔   **cup water**
½   **pound brown-and-serve sausages**
  1   **can (8½ ounces) diagonal-cut green beans, drained**
  1   **can (7 ounces) whole kernel corn, drained**

Remove fat, bone and connective tissue from veal; cube. In large skillet sauté veal in butter until browned; push to one side. Add mushrooms and onion; sauté several minutes. Stir in chicken broth and seasonings. Mix flour and water; add to skillet mixture, stirring until thickened. Cover and simmer for 20 minutes. Cut sausage links in half; brown and drain. Add sausage, green beans and corn to skillet. Cover and simmer an additional 10 minutes. Makes 6 servings.

VEAL-MUSHROOM BUFFET CASSEROLE

½   **cup uncooked rice**
  1   **teaspoon salt**
  1   **cup boiling water**
  1   **pound veal, cut in cubes**
      Vegetable shortening
  1   **package (6 ounces) whole mushrooms frozen in butter sauce in cooking pouch**
1½   **cups chopped celery**
¾   **cup frozen chopped onion**
½   **cup frozen chopped green pepper**
½   **cup chopped pimiento**
  1   **can (10½ ounces) cream of mushroom soup, undiluted**
  3   **tablespoons soy sauce**

Place rice and salt in 1½-quart casserole; add boiling water and set aside. Brown meat in vegetable shortening. Remove frozen mushrooms from pouch. Sauté 5 minutes over high heat in covered skillet. Remove cover; add celery, onion and green pepper and sauté over medium heat for 5 additional minutes. Mix all ingredients with rice in casserole. Cover and bake in preheated oven (350°) for about 1½ hours. Makes 6 servings.

SAUCY BEANS AND FRANKS

- **2 cups canned baked beans**
- **2 cups canned applesauce**
- **¼ cup ketchup**
- **¼ cup chopped onion**
- **¼ cup dark molasses**
- **1 pound frankfurters**

Combine baked beans, applesauce, ketchup, onions and molasses. Pour into a 1-quart casserole. Place frankfurters on top. Cover and bake in preheated oven (375°) 30 to 40 minutes. Makes 4 to 6 servings.

VEAL CUTLET CORDON BLEU

- **12 thin veal cutlets**
- **6 slices Swiss cheese**
- **6 thin slices cooked ham**
- **1 egg**
- **2 tablespoons milk or water**
- **1 teaspoon salt**
- **¼ teaspoon pepper**
- **1 cup flour**
- **1 cup packaged corn flake crumbs**
- **¼ cup shortening**
- **1 package (10 ounces) frozen asparagus spears, cooked**

Pound cutlets until flattened. On 6 cutlets, place one slice each of cheese and ham; top with second cutlet. Lightly beat egg; add milk, salt and pepper. Roll in flour, dip in egg mixture, then roll in corn flake crumbs, coating on all sides. Fry in shortening until brown on both sides, about 6 minutes on each side, adding more shortening if necessary. Serve with hot asparagus spears. Makes 6 servings.

Veal-Mushroom Buffet Casserole

VEAL PAPRIKASH

- 1 pound veal, cut into 1-inch cubes
- 2 tablespoons oil
- 1 cup frozen chopped onion
- ½ cup frozen chopped green pepper
- 1 tablespoon paprika
- 1½ teaspoons salt
- ¼ teaspoon pepper
- 1¾ cups chicken broth, or 2 chicken bouillon cubes dissolved in 1¾ cups hot water
- ¼ cup flour
- ⅓ cup water
- 1 cup dairy sour cream
- 1 package (1 pound) fettucine

Quickly brown veal on all sides in oil. Add onion, green pepper, paprika, salt, pepper and broth. Cook covered over low heat 1 to 1½ hours, or until veal is tender. Blend flour and water. Stir into veal mixture; cook 5 minutes or until thickened, stirring constantly. Stir in sour cream; heat thoroughly, but do not boil. Cook fettucine following package directions; drain. Serve Veal Paprikash spooned over hot fettuccine. Makes 6 servings.

Veal Paprikash

CITY CHICKEN LEGS

- ¾ pound pork tenderloin
- ¾ pound veal steak, cut ½-inch thick
- 1 teaspoon seasoning salt
- ⅛ teaspoon black pepper
- 8 skewers, wooden or metal
- 1 egg, beaten
- 1 tablespoon water
- ½ cup fine dry bread crumbs
- 2 tablespoons shortening
- ¼ cup water
- 1 envelope creamy mushroom gravy mix
- 1 cup milk
- 8 paper frills (optional)

Cut meat into 1½ inch square pieces, about ½ inch thick. Sprinkle pieces with seasoning salt and pepper. Divide pieces of meat to make 8 portions. String pieces on skewer, starting with any smaller pieces, and placing heavier pieces at tip. Push together tightly; with cupped hand round into shape of chicken leg. Combine the beaten egg and water. Dip each leg into mixture then completely cover with crumbs. Brown on all sides in hot shortening. Add ¼ cup water; cover tightly. Cook gently 45 to 60 minutes or until tender. Keep a little water in pan at all times. When finished cooking, place a paper frill, if desired, on the end of each stick. Place on platter. Add mushroom gravy mix to residue in pan. Add milk. Heat to boiling. Spoon over city chicken legs or serve in a gravy boat. Makes 4 servings.

BRAISED PORK CHOPS WITH ONION

- 4 loin pork chops, about 1-inch thick
- 1 tablespoon flour
- 1 tablespoon shortening
- 1 teaspoon salt, divided
- 2 cups frozen chopped onion
- 1 cup sliced celery
- 1 teaspoon poultry seasoning
- ⅛ teaspoon black pepper
- ½ cup water
- 1 envelope brown gravy mix

Sprinkle chops with flour. Brown in hot shortening. Sprinkle with half the salt. Remove chops. Brown onions in fat in skillet, over moderate heat. Add celery. Sprinkle with remaining salt, pepper and poultry seasoning. Stir to distribute seasonings. Tuck chops into onion-celery mixture. Pour over ½ cup of water. Cover tightly. Simmer for 1 hour or until chops are tender. Prepare brown gravy as envelope directs. Serve in gravy boat to spoon over helpings of chops and onion. Makes 4 servings.

City Chicken Legs, Braised Pork Chops with Onion, and Pork with Cabbage

Oriental Spare Ribs

ORIENTAL SPARERIBS

- 2 pounds lean spareribs, cut in serving size pieces
  Seasoned flour
- 1 tablespoon shortening
- 4 cups apple juice
- 1 teaspoon soy sauce.
  Cornstarch
  Fried noodles
  Boiled rice

Roll spareribs in seasoned flour, brown in shortening. Remove spareribs to kettle. Add apple juice; cover and simmer until spareribs are tender, about 1½ to 2 hours. Skim off excess fat. Add soy sauce. Remove spareribs and thicken stock with a little cornstarch mixed to a smooth paste in cold water. Arrange spareribs and gravy on platter. Place boiled rice on one side and fried noodles on other. Makes 4 servings.

PORK WITH CABBAGE

- 1¼ pounds lean pork, pork steak or chops
- 1 tablespoon shortening
- ½ cup frozen chopped onions
- 1 envelope creamy onion sauce mix
- 6 cups finely shredded green cabbage
- 3 cups boiling water
- 1 teaspoon salt
- ¼ cup melted butter

Cut pork into pieces about 1½ inches long, ½ inch thick and ½ inch wide. Brown pieces in hot shortening. Add onions; continue to brown several minutes. Add ½ cup water. Cover tightly; cook over low heat 1 hour. Add ¾ to 1 cup water, depending on amount of liquid left in pan. Add creamy onion sauce mix. Heat to boiling, stirring constantly. Meanwhile, cook cabbage in the boiling water to which the salt has been added. Cook covered 6 to 10 minutes depending on fineness of shred. Drain very well. Add melted butter. Spoon in a circle on platter. Fill center with pork in gravy. Makes 4 servings.

APPLE 'N' SPICE SPARERIBS

- 4 pounds pork spareribs
- 1½ teaspoons salt
- 2 cups canned applesauce
- ⅓ cup light corn syrup
- ¼ teaspoon ground cloves
- ¼ teaspoon paprika

Using kitchen shears, snip meat one-half inch down between tops of rib bones. Fold meat under. Put spareribs, underside up, on rack in broiling pan. Sprinkle with half the salt. Broil 15 minutes on each side. Remove from broiler, pour off fat. Take out rack, place meat back in pan with rounded side up. Sprinkle with remaining salt. Combine applesauce, syrup and cloves. Spoon over meat. Sprinkle with paprika. Bake uncovered in preheated oven (350°) for about 40 minutes, or until ribs are tender. To serve, cut into serving pieces with kitchen shears. Makes 6 servings.

Apple 'N' Spice Spareribs

POT OF GOLD CHOPS

4 pork chops, ¾-inch thick
Salt
Pepper
1 tablespoon shortening
2 cans (1 pound each) cream style golden corn
½ cup frozen chopped onion
1 tablespoon butter

Season chops with salt and pepper. Brown in melted shortening until golden. Combine corn and chopped onion. Place in buttered casserole dish; nestle chops deep into creamed corn mixture. Dot top with butter. Bake uncovered in preheated oven (350°) for about 45 minutes. Makes 4 servings.

SNAPPY WESTERN HAM STEAK

1 slice lean ham steak (pre-cooked)
1 cup mayonnaise
3 tablespoons Hot Dog Relish

Combine relish and mayonnaise. Spread mixture evenly on ham steak. Bake in preheated oven (350°) until relish mixture is firm and ham is heated through, approximately 25 minutes.

SKILLET CHOPS AND RICE

4 chops (pork, lamb or veal), ½-inch thick
Salt and pepper
2 tablespoons cooking oil
½ cup frozen chopped onion
½ cup sliced celery
1½ cups water
2 tablespoons sugar
1½ teaspoon salt
2 cans (8 ounces each) tomato sauce with tomato bits
1 cup regular uncooked rice
1 package (10 ounces) frozen peas, thawed

Sprinkle chops with salt and pepper; brown in oil in skillet. Remove chops. Brown onion and celery in same skillet; add water, sugar, salt and 1 can tomato sauce. Bring to boil. Stir in rice. Place chops in rice mixture; cover tightly and simmer 30 minutes. Add peas and pour on remaining tomato sauce. Cover and simmer 15 more minutes. Makes 4 servings.

Shown opposite:
Corn Medley Casserole
Skillet Supper

Snappy Western Ham Steak, Sweet and Wild Relish, and Smarty Wonderchokes

Savory Lamb Hot Pot

MAIKI HAM

- 1 cup frozen chopped green pepper
- 1 jar (4½ ounces) whole mushrooms, drained
- 3 tablespoons butter, melted
- 1½ pounds cooked ham, cut in 1-inch cubes
- 1 can (20 ounces) pineapple chunks, drained
  Drained pineapple liquid
- 2 tablespoons cornstarch
- ¼ teaspoon salt
- ¼ cup firmly packed brown sugar
- ⅓ cup vinegar
- 2 tablespoons soy sauce

Sauté green pepper and drained mushrooms in melted butter in large heavy frying pan until green pepper is just tender and mushrooms are lightly browned. Add ham and pineapple chunks. Add enough water to pineapple liquid to make 1½ cups; blend in cornstarch and remaining ingredients. Stir into ham-pineapple mixture. Cook over low heat, stirring frequently until slightly thickened, about 10 minutes. Serve over Chinese noodles, if desired. Makes 6 to 8 servings.

SAVORY LAMB HOT POT

- 1 cup finely chopped cooked lamb
- ½ cup frozen chopped onion
- 1 clove garlic, minced
- 3 tablespoons cooking oil
- 1 teaspoon salt
- ⅛ teaspoon pepper
  Dash nutmeg
  Dash savory or basil
- 1 can (8 ounces) tomato sauce
- 2 tablespoons dehydrated parsley flakes
- 2 large zucchini, sliced
- 4 carrots, peeled and sliced
- 2 stalks celery, chopped
- ¼ cup Parmesan cheese

Sauté onion and garlic in oil. Add lamb, salt, pepper, nutmeg, savory, tomato sauce, and parsley. Simmer 10 minutes. In a 2-quart casserole, place half of the lamb mixture, then zucchini, carrots and celery. Top with remaining lamb mixture. Sprinkle with cheese. Bake in preheated oven (375°) for one hour. Makes 4 servings.

Maiki Ham

Shown:
Broiled Round Steak
Cheese Swirled Potatoes
Mustard Steak Sauce
Vegetable Bouquet Salad
Party Apple Creme

EAST-WEST LAMB STEW

¼ cup butter
½ cup frozen chopped onion
1 pound lean lamb, cut in 1½-inch cubes
¾ teaspoon paprika
¾ teaspoon cumin
½ teaspoon cinnamon
¼ teaspoon cloves
½ teaspoon salt
¼ teaspoon pepper
2 cups canned whole peeled tomatoes
1 cup canned garbanzo beans, drained
1 cup canned green beans, small cut, drained
1 cup canned tiny whole boiled onions, drained

Sauté chopped onion in butter in a 2-quart saucepan until transparent; add meat and brown well. Sprinkle with paprika, cumin, cinnamon, cloves, salt and pepper and stir until meat is well coated. Pour tomatoes over meat mixture and cook about 35 minutes, or until meat is fork tender. Add remaining vegetables and cook five minutes or more until vegetables are hot and well covered with sauce. Makes 4 servings.

LAMB SCALLOPINE

2½ pounds lamb shoulder for scallopine
⅓ cup seasoned flour
5 tablespoons oil
2 cups frozen chopped onion
3 cloves garlic, chopped
2 cups tomato juice
1 cup beef bouillon
½ cup dry white wine
1 teaspoon dried rosemary
Cooked green noodles

Pound steaks to about ¼-inch thickness. Dredge steaks in seasoned flour. In a 10-inch aluminum skillet, brown steaks on both sides in oil. Remove meat from pan; keep warm. Add onions and garlic to pan and cook over low heat until onions are soft and golden. Stir in tomato juice, wine and bouillon. Simmer 10 minutes. Add rosemary and browned steaks to the sauce. Simmer, covered, for one hour. To serve, arrange lamb steaks in center of a heated platter. Surround with cooked green noodles. Makes 6 servings.

Lamb Scallopine

Shown:
Mushroom Consomme
Stuffed Baked Potato
Melon—Strawberry Compote

SWEETBREADS A LA POULETTE

- 1 pound sweetbreads
- 1 jar (4½ ounces) sliced mushrooms
- ¼ cup diced green pepper
- 2 tablespoons butter, melted
- 1 package (3 ounces) cream cheese, cubed
- 1 can (10½ ounces) cream of mushroom soup, undiluted
- ¼ teaspoon salt
- 2 cans (7½ ounces each) crab meat, drained and shredded

Simmer sweetbreads in about 1 quart lightly salted water, to which 1 tablespoon vinegar has been added, 20 minutes, or until tender. Drain and cool. Remove membranes and coarsely chop. While sweetbreads are cooking, drain mushrooms, reserving 2 tablespoons mushroom liquid. Sauté green pepper and mushrooms in melted butter, until mushrooms are lightly browned. Add cream cheese and melt over very low heat, stirring frequently. Stir in soup blended with reserved mushroom liquid and salt. Add crab meat and chopped sweetbreads; heat thoroughly. Serve on toast. Makes 6 servings.

CHICKEN MARENGO

- 1 frying chicken, cut up
- ¼ cup flour
- 1 teaspoon salt
- ¼ teaspoon pepper
- 2 tablespoons oil
- 1 clove garlic, crushed
- 1 beef bouillon cube
- ½ cup hot water
- 1 can (4 ounces) mushrooms
- 2 cans (8 ounces each) tomato sauce with tomato bits

Coat chicken with mixture of flour, salt, and pepper. Brown in oil in skillet. Add garlic. Dissolve bouillon cube in hot water; add to skillet along with mushrooms and tomato sauce. Cover and simmer 30 minutes until chicken is tender. Makes 4 servings.

Recipe given for Casserole con Queso and Avocado Corn Dip, shown right, are on page 71 and page 12.

Sweetbreads A La Poulette

CURRIED RICE-CHICKEN CROQUETTES

    1 box (6 ounces) curried rice
    3 tablespoons butter
    ½ cup flour
    1 teaspoon salt
    ¼ teaspoon black pepper
    1¼ cups chicken stock
    1½ teaspoons Worcestershire sauce
    2 cups ground chicken
    1 tablespoon chopped parsley
    ¼ cup chopped green pepper
    2 tablespoons diced pimiento
    1 egg, beaten
    ¼ cup milk
    1 cup dry bread crumbs
    1 package mushroom sauce mix

Cook rice by package directions. Melt butter. Add flour, salt and pepper. Blend until smooth. Stirring constantly, add chicken stock and Worcestershire sauce. Cook until thick. Cool quickly in refrigerator. Add cooked rice, ground chicken, parsley, green pepper and pimiento; mix. Chill. Combine egg and milk. Shape croquettes. Dip in egg-milk mixture. Roll in dry bread crumbs. Deep fat fry at 360° for approximately 5 minutes. Serve immediately with prepared mushroom sauce. Makes 6 to 8 servings.

CHICKEN ROOS COMBOLLO

    1 frying chicken, cut in serving pieces
      Flour
      Salt
      Pepper
    4 tablespoons olive oil
    1 cup frozen chopped onion
    ½ green pepper, chopped
    1 clove garlic, crushed
    1½ cups chicken broth
    2 cans (14 ounces each) wild rice

Dredge chicken with flour, salt and pepper and brown in olive oil. Remove chicken and sauté onions, pepper and garlic in same pan for five minutes. Return chicken to the pan, add chicken broth, cover and cook over low heat until chicken is almost done (about 30 minutes). Spread drained wild rice in a shallow casserole dish. Arrange chicken pieces on top and pour the stock remaining (there should be about 1 cup) over the chicken. Cover and bake in preheated oven (350°) for 20 to 30 minutes. Makes 3 to 4 servings.

Recipes for Chive Rice and Creamed Chipped Beef, shown opposite, are on pages 39 and 73.

Curried Rice-Chicken Croquettes

WILD RICE-CHICKEN SUPREME

1 box (6 ounces) long grain & wild rice
¼ cup butter
⅓ cup frozen chopped onion
⅓ cup all-purpose flour
1 teaspoon salt
  Pepper to taste
1 cup half-and-half cream
1 cup chicken broth
2 cups cooked, cubed chicken
⅓ cup chopped pimiento
⅓ cup chopped parsley
3 tablespoons chopped, blanched almonds

Cook rice according to directions on package. Sauté the onions in butter. Add flour, salt and pepper; blend. Stirring constantly, add cream and chicken broth gradually. Cook until thickened. Add sauce, chicken, pimiento, parsley and almonds to cooked rice and mix well. Pour into a greased baking pan. Bake in preheated oven (425°) for 30 minutes. Makes 6 to 8 servings.

CRANBERRY ROSE CHICKEN

1 broiling chicken, cut in serving pieces
  Salt and pepper
1 cup commercial cranberry-orange relish
½ cup applesauce
½ cup rose wine
¼ cup commercial Italian salad dressing

Season chicken with salt and pepper. Place pieces in a shallow pan. Combine remaining ingredients; stir until well blended. Pour mixture over the chicken and let stand in refrigerator for several hours or overnight. Drain chicken and broil for about 20 minutes, basting occasionally with remaining marinade. Spoon heated marinade over chicken before serving. Makes 3 to 4 servings.

CRANBERRY GLAZED TURKEY ROLL

1 boned turkey roll (5 to 7 pounds), thawed
1 can (8 ounces) cranberry sauce
¼ cup brown sugar
¼ teaspoon cinnamon

Arrange turkey roll in a small roasting pan. In a saucepan, heat cranberry sauce, brown sugar, and cinnamon until sauce and sugar are melted; stir occasionally. Paint turkey roll with this glaze. Roast in preheated oven (350°) for 2½ to 3 hours. Baste with glaze several times during roasting. Remove roast to platter and garnish with parsley and the contents of a jar of spiced apple rings, if desired. Makes 8 servings.

BARBECUED CHICKEN WITH SOUR CREAM-CHERVIL SAUCE

1 broiler chicken, cut in parts
1 package instant meat marinade
½ pint dairy sour cream
1 tablespoon lemon juice
½ teaspoon chervil

Pour contents of instant meat marinade into a shallow pan. Thoroughly blend in remaining ingredients. Place chicken pieces in marinade; coat all sides thoroughly. Remove chicken, reserve marinade. Place chicken on grill over hot coals, or under a broiler. Grill for 40 minutes, basting frequently and turning occasionally. Makes 3 servings.

ORANGE NUGGET ROAST TURKEY

1 8- to 10-pound ready-to-cook turkey
5 medium California oranges, unpeeled
3 slices day-old bread, torn in small pieces
¼ teaspoon salt
  Dash pepper

Rinse turkey, drain and pat dry with paper towels. Cut 3 oranges into chunks, combine with bread pieces and seasonings. Spoon orange chunk mixture into neck and body cavities of turkey. Close cavities with skewers. Place turkey, breast side up, on rack in shallow roasting pan. Cover breastbone area only with strip of aluminum foil. Roast in preheated oven (325°) approximately 3 to 4 hours, or until meat thermometer inserted in thickest part of breast or thigh registers 180 to 185 degrees. While turkey is roasting, squeeze juice from remaining oranges, and use for basting turkey during roasting. When done, remove orange stuffing and discard; flavor and fragrance has already penetrated turkey. Allow turkey to "rest" 30 minutes for easier carving. Makes 8 servings.

Shown: Cranberry Glazed Turkey Roll, Cauliflower Pane, Peas Aux Herbes, Red Hot Tureen, Roquefort Dressing, and Party Tarts.

Desserts

FRUIT WITH CHUTNEY DIP

- 1 package (8 ounces) cream cheese
- ½ cup finely chopped chutney
- ¼ cup dry sherry wine
- 2 tablespoons finely chopped green onion
- 4 teaspoons old fashion French salad dressing mix
- ½ cup dairy sour cream
- 2 teaspoons lemon juice
  Assorted fruit (melon wedges, melon balls, blueberries, pear wedges, and apple slices)

Soften cream cheese. Blend in chutney, sherry, onion, and salad dressing mix. Add sour cream and lemon juice, blending well. Chill and serve with assorted fruit platter. Makes about 2 cups of dip.

COFFEE PEACH FRAPPÉ

- 3 tablespoons instant coffee
- 1½ cups cold water
- ½ cup bourbon
- 1 can (1 pound) sliced peaches, chilled
- ⅛ teaspoon nutmeg
- 1 pint vanilla ice cream, divided
  Crushed ice

Dissolve coffee in cold water in a medium bowl; stir in bourbon. Set aside. In electric blender, combine peaches with syrup, nutmeg, and about 1½ cups of the ice cream. Blend on high speed until smooth. Pour over reserved coffee mixture and stir until blended. Serve in tall glasses over crushed ice, or pour into punch cups. Top each with a small scoop of the remaining ice cream. Makes about 5 servings.

Shown at left:
Fruit with Chutney Dip
Coffee Peach Frappe

MELON-STRAWBERRY COMPOTE

- 1 package frozen melon balls
- 1 pint strawberries, frozen whole
- 1 cup lemon-lime carbonated soda
  Mint leaves

Combine semi-defrosted melon and strawberries. Pour lemon-lime soda over and lightly toss. Spoon into eight sherbet glasses and garnish with fresh mint leaves. Makes 8 servings.

FESTIVE FRUIT PLATTER

- 1 fresh pineapple
- 1 pint strawberries
- 1 package (1 pound) California dates
- 1 bag (12 ounces) dried apricots
- 1 large bunch green grapes
- 2 apples, cut into wedges and sprinkled with lemon juice
- 2 papayas, pared and sliced
- 1 package (1 pound) Calimyrna figs

Cut wedge out of pineapple and cut meat into bite sized pieces. Line a large serving platter with greens. Place pineapple in center and arrange pieces of pineapple and other fruits around base. Makes 8 servings.

BAKED PEARS WITH PORT

- 6 ripe Bartlett or Anjou pears
- 1 cup sugar
- ½ cup Port wine
- 1 teaspoon butter

Wash pears and remove the blossom ends. Scoop out core or not, as you wish. Heat sugar and wine together until sugar is dissolved; add butter, and pour over pears. Cover and bake in preheated oven (350°) 1 hour, or until pears are tender. Makes 6 servings.

Walnut Chocolate Pear Cream

WALNUT CHOCOLATE PEAR CREAM

  1 package (6 ounces) semi-sweet chocolate
      morsels
 ½ cup light corn syrup
  1 cup coarsely chopped walnuts
  3 cups canned pears
  1 cup heavy cream
 ½ cup dairy sour cream
  2 teaspoons vanilla

Melt semi-sweet chocolate morsels and syrup together in top of double boiler; stir in chopped walnuts. Set aside to cool slightly. Drain and cut up pears. Whip cream stiff and fold in sour cream and vanilla. Gently mix in cooled chocolate-walnut mixture and pears. Chill for several hours before serving. Spoon into individual dessert dishes and decorate with toasted walnut halves, if desired. Makes 8 to 10 servings.

FLAMING PINEAPPLE RUMBA

  1 can (1 pound, 14 ounces) pineapple slices
      Cinnamon
 ¼ cup butter
  1 cup apricot pineapple preserves
 ½ cup dark rum
      Vanilla or coconut ice cream

Drain pineapple well and sprinkle lightly with cinnamon. Reserve 6 tablespoons syrup. Melt butter in top pan or blazer of chafing dish placed directly over flame. When butter is bubbly hot, add pineapple and sauté until edges are browned. Push to side of pan. Stir in preserves and reserved pineapple syrup. Heat and spoon over pineapple until it looks glazed and transparent. Heat rum over hot water, then pour over fruit. Ignite and spoon flaming sauce over pineapple. When flame dies down, arrange pineapple around scoops of hard ice cream. Spoon hot sauce over top. Makes 8 servings.

RUM DUFF

2 cups canned applesauce
¼ cup sugar
3 tablespoons rum (or 1 teaspoon rum extract)
1 tablespoon grated orange rind
2 cups broken gingersnaps
½ cup heavy cream, whipped

Combine applesauce, sugar, rum, grated orange rind and gingersnaps. Stir until well mixed. Chill. Just before serving fold in whipped cream. Pile into sherbet glasses. Makes 6 to 8 servings. If desired, top with additional whipped cream and a sprinkle of chopped nuts.

French Orange Custard

FRESH ORANGE CUSTARD

1 package (4⅛ ounces) no-bake egg custard
    mix
2½ cups milk
4 large oranges
⅔ cup malted cereal granules, or
    flaked coconut, or
    chopped pecans or walnuts, or
    sliced maraschino cherries

Prepare custard mix according to package directions, using 2½ cups milk. Chill custard until cool, but not set. Cut peeled oranges into bite-size pieces; drain thoroughly. Place orange pieces in sherbet glasses or custard cups. Sprinkle each with about 1 tablespoon of the suggested cereal, nuts, cherries, etc. Pour cooled custard over oranges; chill until set. If desired, garnish with additional cereal, cherries, etc. Makes 6 servings.

PRINCESS PARFAIT

1 quart vanilla ice cream (softened)
1 can fruit cocktail, drained
    Crème de menthe
    Grenadine
½ pint heavy cream
8 maraschino cherries with stems

In eight parfait glasses, place a small scoop of vanilla ice cream in bottom of each glass, then a layer of drained fruit cocktail, another scoop of ice cream, then another layer of fruit cocktail. Pour crème de menthe and a little grenadine over; add a dollop of whipped cream and top with a cherry. These can be made ahead of time and stored in freezer for a few hours. Makes 8 servings.

Strawberry Cream Crown

STRAWBERRY-CREAM CROWN

1 quart fresh strawberries
½ cup peach flavored brandy
1 package (3 ounces) vanilla pudding
½ cup heavy cream, whipped
1 cup dairy sour cream
 Lady fingers

Wash, hull and cut strawberries in half. Mix together with peach flavored brandy. Refrigerate 4 hours or overnight. Prepare vanilla pudding according to package directions and chill. To serve, fold vanilla pudding, whipped cream and sour cream into strawberries. Put in a bowl and surround with lady fingers. Makes 6 servings.

SAUCY-RASPBERRY DESSERT

1 package raspberry flavored gelatin
1 cup hot water
1 cup canned applesauce
2 tablespoons sugar
1 teaspoon grated lemon rind
1 tablespoon lemon juice
⅔ cup chopped walnuts
¾ cup tiny marshmallows
¾ cup heavy cream, whipped

Dissolve raspberry gelatin in hot water. Add applesauce, sugar, lemon rind and juice. Chill over ice water until slightly thickened. Fold in walnuts and marshmallows. Pour into a 1-quart mold. Chill until firm. Unmold and serve with whipped cream. Makes 6 servings.

Saucy Raspberry Dessert

WALNUT DELIGHT

1 package yellow cake mix
1 cup chopped walnuts
4 egg whites
Pinch of salt
1 cup sugar

Prepare cake mix according to package directions and spoon into greased and floured 9-inch layer cake pans. Sprinkle walnuts evenly over both layers. (If sprinkled only around edges, cake will hump in the center; if sprinkled only in center, it sinks.) Beat egg whites with salt until foamy; add sugar gradually and beat until stiff, but still shiny, peaks form. This should be a stiff meringue as for a torte, not a soft meringue as for a pie. Spread evenly over both layers, but do not seal to edge of pans. Bake in preheated oven (350°) for 35 to 40 minutes. (This is 10 minutes more than package directions call for.) Cool on rack in pans 5 minutes; then turn out and complete cooling. Meringue will settle, forming a basket for filling.

FILLING

4 egg yolks
¼ teaspoon salt
½ cup sugar
¼ cup lemon juice
1 teaspoon grated lemon rind

Beat egg yolks and salt until thick and lemon-colored. Gradually beat in sugar and continue beating until very thick. Stir in lemon juice and rind. Cook over hot water, stirring constantly, until thick, 5 to 8 minutes. Cool. Put layers together with this filling.

FROSTING

1½ cups heavy cream
1 teaspoon vanilla
2 dozen walnut halves

Whip cream with vanilla until stiff. Spread and swirl over cake. Decorate with walnut halves. Makes one 9-inch layer cake.

Apple Orange Cake

APPLE ORANGE CAKE

2½ cups canned apple slices
¼ cup butter
1 cup light brown sugar
Dash cinnamon
1 package yellow cake mix
Orange juice
2 tablespoons grated orange rind
Whipped cream
Nutmeg

Drain apples. Melt butter in 12" x 8" x 2" pan; sprinkle with brown sugar and cinnamon. Arrange apples in rows on sugar mixture. Prepare cake mix according to directions on package, substituting orange juice for the liquid called for in the recipe. Add grated orange rind. Pour batter over apples in pan. Bake in preheated oven (375°) 40 minutes. Cool 10 minutes in pan. Turn upside down on serving plate. Serve hot or cold with whipped cream, topped with dash of nutmeg. Makes about 12 servings.

PARTY APPLE CREME

1 cup apple juice
1 package (3 ounces) raspberry flavor gelatin
1 pint softened vanilla ice cream
2 cups canned applesauce

Heat apple juice to boiling. Combine with gelatin in a 1½-quart bowl and stir to dissolve gelatin. Blend in ice cream. Fold in 1½ cups applesauce. Chill until mixture is thickened. Spoon into bowl and garnish with remaining applesauce. Makes 8 servings.

SHIMMERING MINT MOLD

2 cans (1 pound each) applesauce
4 two-serving envelopes of low-calorie lime gelatin
2 tablespoons crème de menthe

In a saucepan, heat applesauce to boiling point. Sprinkle gelatin over surface of applesauce, stirring to blend thoroughly. Simmer applesauce until all gelatin is dissolved. Stir in crème de menthe; simmer 1 minute longer. Pour into mold; chill until firm. Makes 8 servings.

BANANA SPICE CAKE WITH QUICK SOUR CREAM TOPPING

Cake:
1 package banana cake mix
1¼ cups water
2 eggs, unbeaten
½ teaspoon ground cinnamon
¼ teaspoon ground nutmeg
¼ teaspoon ground cloves
Topping:
1 cup dairy sour cream
⅓ cup firmly packed brown sugar
⅓ cup chopped walnuts

Place cake mix in mixing bowl; add water, eggs, and spices. Blend at low speed just to moisten. Beat 3 minutes at medium speed of mixer or with spoon until creamy. Pour batter into 13" x 9" pan, which has been greased and floured on bottom and sides. Bake in preheated oven (350°) for 40 to 45 minutes. Meanwhile, combine sour cream with brown sugar. When cake is done, remove from oven, spread with sour cream mixture and sprinkle with walnuts. Return to oven and bake 5 minutes longer. Cool and cut into squares.

CHOCOLATE WALNUT SAUCE

½ cup butter
2 cups chopped walnuts
2 cups semi-sweet chocolate morsels

Melt butter in a heavy skillet. Add walnuts and cook over medium heat, stirring constantly, until browned. Remove from heat. Add semi-sweet chocolate morsels and stir until smooth. Serve warm over ice cream or warm cake squares. Makes 2½ cups.

Banana Spice Cake With Sour Cream Topping

Fudge Frost 'N' Bake Cake

FUDGE FROST 'N' BAKE CAKE

1 cup semi-sweet chocolate morsels
⅔ cup sweetened condensed milk
2 tablespoons water
1 teaspoon vanilla
1 package white or yellow cake mix
½ cup nuts

Melt semi-sweet chocolate morsels over hot (not boiling) water. Remove from heat. Add condensed milk, water and vanilla, stirring until smooth. Line bottom and sides of 12" x 8" x 2" baking dish each way with double thicknesses of waxed paper. Pour in chocolate mixture. Prepare cake mix according to label directions. Pour gently over chocolate mixture. Bake at oven temperature recommended in package directions until cake tests done (longer baking is required). Invert cake on rack. Lift off baking dish. Let stand 2 minutes. Peel off paper. Press nuts in hot frosting. Cool. Cut in approximately 2-inch squares. Makes 15 squares.

Chocolate Chip Petits Fours, Butter Cream Frosting, and Chocolate Glaze

Refrigerator Cheese Cake

REFRIGERATOR CHEESE CAKE

CRUST

1 cup fine graham cracker crumbs
¼ cup butter, melted

Blend together. Press ⅔ of mixture firmly on bottom of 8-inch spring form pan. Chill, reserving remainder of crumbs for top crust.

CHEESE CAKE

2 tablespoons unflavored gelatin
¼ cup cold water
2 eggs separated
¼ cup milk
1 teaspoon salt
¼ cup heavy cream, whipped
1 teaspoon vanilla
½ cup sugar
2 cups (1 lb.) cottage cheese, sieved
1 can (6-ounce) frozen orange juice, thawed and undiluted

Blend unflavored gelatin and water in small saucepan and melt over low heat. Remove from heat and cool slightly. Combine egg yolks, slightly beaten, with milk, salt and sugar, in top part of double boiler. Stir over hot water until mixture thickens. It must not boil. Remove from hot water. Stir in melted gelatin. Mix well and place pan in bowl of cold water, stirring constantly. When mixture is cool, remove from water and add sieved cottage cheese, concentrated orange juice, and vanilla. Fold in whipped cream. Beat egg whites until stiff, not dry, and fold into mixture. Pour mixture into prepared pan. Sprinkle with remaining crumbs. Chill for 2 hours. Serves 8.

LEMON COCONUT WHIP

1 package Whip 'n' Chill Lemon Dessert Mix
2 tablespoons sugar
1 cup dairy sour cream
½ teaspoon grated lemon rind
¼ cup shredded coconut

Combine dessert mix and sugar. Prepare mix as directed on the package. Blend in sour cream, grated lemon rind and coconut. Chill for at least 2 hours. Makes 6 servings.

CHOCOLATE CHIP PETITS FOURS

1 package fudge coconut cake mix
1¼ cups water
2 eggs, unbeaten
Butter Cream Frosting (recipe follows)
Chocolate Glaze (recipe follows)

Prepare cake mix with water and eggs as directed on package, baking in a 13" x 9" pan. Cool in pan 10 minutes; turn out onto rack to finish cooling. Prepare Butter Cream Frosting as directed; spread over top of cake. Cut cake in half. Prepare Chocolate Glaze as directed; drizzle over one cake half. Cut both halves into bars or squares. Decorate unglazed cake with toasted coconut, candied fruits, or silver dragees, if desired.

BUTTER CREAM FROSTING

½ cup butter
⅛ teaspoon salt
4 cups sifted confectioners' sugar
2 egg yolks, unbeaten (or 1 whole egg)
1 teaspoon vanilla
2 tablespoons milk (about)

Cream butter until soft. Add salt and half of the sugar gradually, blending after each addition. Then add egg yolks and vanilla; blend well. Add remaining sugar alternately with milk until of right consistency to spread, beating after each addition until smooth. Makes about 2½ cups.

CHOCOLATE GLAZE

1 cup sifted confectioners' sugar
1 package unsweetened product for chocolate baking
2 tablespoons (about) hot milk.

Sift sugar into a small bowl. Gradually stir in unsweetened product for chocolate baking and milk until glaze is of right consistency for spreading. Makes about ⅓ cup.

Blueberry Rice Supreme

BLUEBERRY RICE SUPREME

- ⅔ cup packaged pre-cooked rice
- ¼ teaspoon salt
- ⅔ cup boiling water
- 1½ cups fresh blueberries
- ½ cup flaked coconut
- ⅓ cup chopped walnuts
- 1 cup heavy cream
- ¼ cup granulated sugar
- ½ teaspoon almond extract

Prepare rice with salt and water as directed on package, then remove cover and let cool to room temperature. Mix blueberries, coconut, walnuts, and cooled rice. Whip cream; add sugar and almond extract. Fold into rice mixture. Chill about 1 hour. Serve with additional coconut or the new packaged toasted coconut, if desired. Makes 8 servings.

GOLDEN BRANDY PUFF

- 1 cup light brown sugar
- 1 cup chopped walnuts
- 1 cup light seedless raisins
- 2 cups canned applesauce
- ½ cup apricot brandy
- 2 teaspoons cinnamon
- ½ teaspoon nutmeg
- ¼ teaspoon ginger
- 4 egg whites
- ½ cup granulated sugar

Combine light brown sugar, walnuts, raisins, applesauce, apricot brandy, cinnamon, nutmeg and ginger in a saucepan. Bring to a boil, stirring occasionally. Spoon into a 6-cup baking dish. Beat egg whites with a rotary beater until soft peaks form. Gradually add sugar and beat until stiff. Pile lightly on top of pudding in baking dish. Bake in a 325° oven 15 to 20 minutes or until meringue is a delicate brown. Serve at once. Makes 6 servings.

FROZEN BERRY REFRIGERATOR CAKE

- 2 packages (10 ounces each) frozen strawberries in syrup, thawed
- 2 envelopes unflavored gelatin
- ½ cup cold water
- 1 package (8 ounces) cream cheese, softened at room temperature
- ¼ cup sugar
- 1 package ladyfingers (about 16)
  Whipped Cream Frozen Berry Sauce (recipe follows)

Drain syrup from berries into a 1-quart measure. Add water to make 3 cups. Sprinkle gelatin on cold water and let stand 5 minutes. Combine softened gelatin and syrup mixture in saucepan; heat, stirring, until gelatin is dissolved. Beat cream cheese and sugar until soft and fluffy. Gradually beat gelatin mixture into cream cheese. Chill until mixture thickens. Beat with a rotary beater or electric mixer until mixture is fluffy. Fold in reserved berries. Arrange split lady fingers, rounded side out, on bottom and around sides of a 9 x 5 x 3-inch loaf pan. Spoon half the gelatin mixture into prepared pan. Top with a layer of split ladyfingers. Add remaining gelatin mixture. Chill until firm. To serve, invert on serving platter and top with whipped cream. Serve with Frozen Berry Sauce.

FROZEN BERRY SAUCE

- 1 package frozen strawberries in syrup, thawed
- 2 teaspoons cornstarch
- 1 tablespoon water.

Drain syrup from berries into saucepan. Bring to a boil over low heat. Blend together cornstarch and cold water. Add to syrup and simmer and stir, until clear and thickened. Add berries. Chill.

Frozen Berry Refrigerator Cake

Golden Brandy Puff

Apple Nut Drops

Apple Cheese Quiche Pie

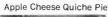

APPLE NUT DROPS

½ cup shortening
⅔ cup sugar
2 eggs
1 cup sifted flour
1 teaspoon baking powder
1 teaspoon cinnamon
½ teaspoon nutmeg
½ teaspoon ground cloves
½ teaspoon salt
1 cup rolled oats
1 cup chopped, canned apple slices, well drained
1 cup chopped walnut meats

Cream together shortening and sugar. Add eggs, one at a time, beating after each. Sift together flour, baking powder, cinnamon, nutmeg, ground cloves and salt; mix with oats. Add alternately with apples to creamed mixture. Add walnuts; mix well. Drop by rounded tablespoons on greased baking sheet. Bake in preheated oven (350 degrees) 15 to 18 minutes. Makes about 3 dozen cookies.

SURPRISE APPLE CRISP

- 2 cans (1 pound each) apple pie slices
- 1 package (6 ounces) butterscotch flavored morsels
- 2 tablespoons quick-cooking tapioca
- 1 tablespoon lemon juice
- ½ cup unsifted, all-purpose flour
- ½ cup sugar
- 1 teaspoon cinnamon
- ½ cup firm, cold butter

Combine apples, all but 1 tablespoon butterscotch flavored morsels and tapioca in 1½-quart casserole; mix well. Sprinkle with lemon juice. Mix flour, sugar and cinnamon in bowl; cut in butter. Crumble over apple mixture. Bake in preheated oven (375°) 40 minutes. Sprinkle with remaining butterscotch morsels and bake 5 minutes longer. Serve warm with cream or ice cream, if desired. Makes 6 servings.

APPLE CHEESE QUICHE PIE

- 1 package pie crust mix
- 1 package (6 ounces) sliced natural Swiss cheese
- 2 cups canned applesauce
- 3 eggs, well beaten
- 1 tablespoon flour
- ½ teaspoon salt
  Dash pepper
- ⅛ teaspoon ground nutmeg
- 1 cup milk or light cream

Prepare pie crust according to directions on package. Roll out pastry until large enough to line the bottom and sides of an ungreased 10-inch pie pan, fluting a high edge. Cut cheese slices into halves and use cheese to line the bottom and sides of the pie shell. Spread applesauce evenly in pie shell. Beat eggs with flour, salt, pepper and nutmeg. Gradually beat in milk or cream. Pour mixture over applesauce. Bake in preheated oven (375°) 40 to 45 minutes or until custard is set and the top is richly browned. Cool slightly and then cut into wedges. If desired, serve with warm applesauce. Makes 6 to 8 servings.

Surprise Apple Crisp

WALNUT RAISIN BABA

1 package date bar mix
⅔ cup hot water
3 eggs
¼ cup sifted flour
¾ teaspoon baking powder
½ teaspoon salt
2 tablespoons light molasses
1 teaspoon cinnamon
¼ teaspoon nutmeg
¼ teaspoon allspice
1 cup dark or golden raisins
1 cup chopped candied fruit
1 cup chopped walnuts
    Rum syrup (recipe follows)
    Fruited Hard Sauce (recipe follows)

Combine date filling from date bar mix package with hot water. Add crumbly mix, eggs, flour, baking powder, salt, molasses and spices. Beat well, stir in raisins, candied fruits and walnuts. Spoon into greased and floured 1½-quart ring mold. Bake in preheated oven (325°) for 45 minutes. Remove from oven and let cake stand in pan 5 minutes. Turn out on serving plate. Slowly spoon on warm Rum Syrup so it will absorb into cake. Serve hot with Fruited Hard Sauce. Makes 10 servings.

RUM SYRUP

½ cup light corn syrup
2 tablespoons water
1 tablespoon lemon juice
    Salt
2 tablespoons light rum

In a saucepan, combine syrup, water, lemon juice, and a few grains of salt. Bring to boil, lower heat and simmer 3 or 4 minutes. Remove from heat and add rum.

FRUITED HARD SAUCE

¼ cup soft butter
2 cups sifted confectioners' sugar
1 tablespoon cream
1 tablespoon lemon juice
¼ cup chopped seedless raisins
¼ cup candied fruit
⅓ cup chopped walnuts

Cream together butter, sugar and cream until smooth. Add lemon juice, raisins, and fruit. Shape into a roll about 1½" diameter; wrap in waxed paper and chill until firm. Remove paper and roll hard sauce in chopped walnuts. Cut in slices to serve.

PINK SHOWER CAKE

1 package lemon flake cake mix
2 egg whites, unbeaten
1½ cups sugar
½ teaspoon cream of tartar
2 teaspoons vanilla
½ cup boiling water
    Red food coloring

Prepare cake mix as directed on package, baking in one 9-inch square pan. When cake has cooled, split into 2 layers; then fill and frost with Pink Frosting.

To make Pink Frosting, combine egg whites, sugar, cream of tartar, and vanilla in mixing bowl; mix well. Add boiling water and beat at high speed of electric mixer or with rotary beater until mixture will stand in stiff peaks, 10 to 12 minutes. Add a few drops of food coloring; blend in thoroughly. Makes 5 cups frosting. Store uncovered cake in refrigerator to prevent frosting from becoming too soft.

Walnut Raisin Baba

Pink Shower Cake

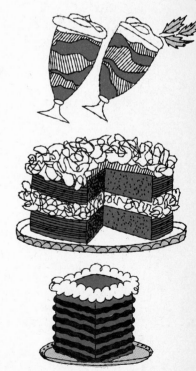

MERINGUE-CAPPED APRICOT TARTLETS

1 pan Brown 'N Serve Butter Tea Rolls
1 egg, separated
¼ cup heavy cream
1 teaspoon vanilla
2 tablespoons sugar
20 unpeeled apricot halves
1 egg white
⅓ cup sugar, divided
2 tablespoons slivered almonds

Remove ten of the rolls from the pan, separate, and halve them horizontally with a sharp knife. Beat egg yolk with the cream, vanilla and two tablespoons of sugar, and dip cut sides of rolls in this mixture. Place drained apricot, cut side up, on dipped side of roll. Place on ungreased baking sheet and bake in preheated oven (350°) for 8 minutes. Meantime, make a meringue by beating the two egg whites with the remaining sugar until very stiff. Remove baking sheet from oven and cap each tartlet with a tablespoon of the meringue. Decorate with slivered almonds and bake for 7 more minutes until meringue and almonds are delicately browned. Serve hot or cold. Makes 20 Apricot Tartlets.

FROSTED DATE ROLL-UPS

1 package hot roll mix
1 cup dates, cut-up
1 cup confectioners' sugar
4 teaspoons warm water

Prepare hot roll mix according to directions on the package. Roll out to ¼-inch thickness. Sprinkle surface with cut-up dates. Roll up as a jelly roll. Cut in 1½-inch slices. Place slices cut side up, in muffin tins. Bake according to directions on the package. Remove from oven; cool. Drizzle with sugar frosting made by stirring warm water into lump-free confectioners' sugar; blend until smooth. Makes 12 large or 24 small rolls.

MARASCHINO NUT LOAF

1 cup sugar
2 eggs
1 jar (8 ounce) red maraschino cherries
1 cup milk or syrup from cherries with enough milk to make 1 cup
3 cups pre-sifted flour
4 teaspoons double action baking powder
2 tablespoons butter, melted and cooled
½ cup walnuts, chopped

Beat eggs and sugar. Add cherries and milk. Add flour, baking powder; then add melted cooled butter. Add chopped nuts. Pour into well greased 9" x 5" x 2-¾" loaf pan and bake in oven at 350 degrees for approximately one hour or until toothpick inserted in center of loaf comes out clean. The top of the loaf will be irregular. Makes 6 to 8 servings.

DATE NUT BARS

4 eggs, well beaten
2½ cups firmly packed light brown sugar
1 tall can (1⅔ cups) evaporated milk
2 tablespoons lemon juice
2½ cups sifted flour
1½ teaspoons baking soda
1 teaspoon cinnamon
½ teaspoon salt
1½ cups chopped pecans
1½ cups chopped dates
Sifted confectioners sugar

In a large mixing bowl combine beaten eggs, brown sugar, evaporated milk and lemon juice. Sift together flour, soda, cinnamon and salt. Add all at once to egg mixture. Stir just until blended. Fold in pecans and dates, being careful not to overmix. Spread batter in two well-greased jelly roll pans, 15½ x 10½ x 1-inch. Bake at 350 degrees for 20 minutes. Set pans on racks to cool. Sprinkle with confectioners sugar; cut into bars. Makes 5 dozen bars.

Meringue-Capped Apricot Tartlets

Maraschino Nut Loaf

Chocolate Mousse

CHOCOLATE MOUSSE

  1 envelope unflavored gelatin
⅔ cup sugar, divided
½ cup water
  1 package (6 ounces) semi-sweet chocolate
    morsels
  4 eggs, separated
  1 teaspoon vanilla
¼ teaspoon salt
  1 cup heavy cream, whipped

Combine unflavored gelatin, ⅓ cup of the sugar
and water in saucepan. Place over low heat,
stirring until gelatin and sugar are dissolved.
Add semi-sweet chocolate morsels and continue
stirring until dissolved. Remove from heat. Beat
in egg yolks and vanilla. Beat egg whites and
salt until stiff but not dry. Gradually add remaining ⅓ cup sugar; beat until very stiff. Fold
in chocolate mixture thoroughly; then fold in
whipped cream. Spoon into dessert dishes. Chill
until firm. If desired, garnish with additional
whipped cream, kumquats and toasted almonds.
Makes 8 servings.

Lemon-Filled Banana Cup Cakes

Fruit Stollen

LEMON-FILLED BANANA CUPCAKES

> 1 **package banana cake mix**
> **Lemon Beat 'n Eat Frosting (recipe follows)**
> ⅔ **cup red jelly**

Prepare cake mix as directed, baking in cupcake pans. When cool, carefully cut a cone shape from the top of each cupcake. Fill with Lemon Beat 'n Eat Frosting. Dot with jelly, using about 1 teaspoon for each. Place cones back on cakes on top of frosting. Store uncovered at room temperature or uncovered in refrigerator. Makes 30 to 36 filled cupcakes.

LEMON BEAT 'n EAT FROSTING

> 2 **egg whites, unbeaten**
> 1½ **cups sugar**
> ½ **teaspoon cream of tartar**
> ½ **cup boiling water**
> 2 **teaspoons lemon juice**
> 1 **teaspoon grated lemon rind**

Combine egg whites, sugar, and cream of tartar in mixing bowl; mix well. Add boiling water and beat at high speed of electric mixer or with rotary beater until mixture forms stiff peaks, about 10 to 12 minutes. Stir in lemon juice and rind. Makes 5 cups frosting.

FRUIT STOLLEN

> 1 **package hot roll mix**
> 1 **tablespoon sugar**
> 2 **cups glace cake mixed fruits**
> 1 **cup sifted confectioners' sugar, sifted**
> 4 **to 5 tablespoons milk or fruit juice**

Prepare hot roll mix according to package directions adding 1 tablespoon sugar. Add an egg if not included in your package directions. Mix half the fruit glace into the dough. Shape dough into 11 or 12 round balls and place side by side on cookie sheet to form wreath. Let rise until double in bulk. Bake in preheated oven (375°) until golden brown, about 20 to 25 minutes. Glaze while still warm with mixture of powdered sugar and milk or juice. Decorate with remaining fruit glace. Serve warm.

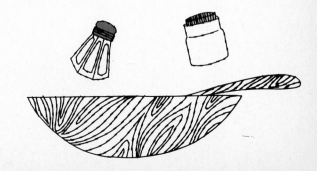

CHOCOLATE REFRIGERATOR CAKE

1 package (6 ounces) semi-sweet chocolate
    morsels
1½ tablespoons water
4 eggs, separated
1 teaspoon vanilla
1 cup heavy cream
    Angel food cake

Melt chocolate in top of double boiler over hot (not boiling) water. Add water and stir until chocolate appears smooth. Add egg yolks one at a time, beating well after each addition. Stir in vanilla. Beat egg whites until stiff but not dry. Fold into chocolate mixture. Whip cream until it holds soft peaks and fold into chocolate mixture. Line bottom of a cake or bread loaf pan with thin slices of angel food cake. Top with half the chocolate mixture. Add another layer of angel food, top with remaining chocolate. Put in refrigerator several hours or overnight. (Do not freeze.) Loosen with knife from sides of pan and unmold. Slice to serve.

TORTE ANGELIQUE

1 package instant chocolate pudding
1 pint heavy cream
    8-inch angel food cake

Mix chocolate pudding with cream. Let mixture stand until pudding is dissolved; then whip. Cut cake into 3 layers. Spread mixture between layers and over outside of cake. Place in freezing compartment for several hours before serving. Makes 6 servings.

Chocolate Chip Cake Brownies

CHOCOLATE CHIP CAKE BROWNIES

1 package chocolate chip cake mix, divided
⅓ cup water
1 egg
¼ cup softened butter
1 cup chopped walnuts

Place about half of the cake mix in mixing bowl. Add water, egg, and butter. Beat well with wooden spoon. Add remaining mix and nuts; blend thoroughly. Pour batter into generously greased and floured 8-inch square pans. Bake in preheated oven (375°) for 20 to 25 minutes. Cool; then cut in bars. Makes about 32 bars.

APPLE CHIP DROP COOKIES

1 package apple chip cake mix, divided
½ cup soft shortening
1 tablespoon water
2 eggs
½ cup dark seedless raisins
½ cup chopped pecans

Empty half of cake mix into bowl. Add shortening, water, and eggs; blend well. Then add remaining mix, the raisins, and nuts; beat until smooth. Drop by teaspoonsful onto greased baking sheets. Bake in preheated oven (375°) for 10 minutes, or until lightly browned. Store in airtight container. Makes about 4 dozen cookies.

CREAMY CHOCOLATE FROSTING

- 1 package cupcake mix
- 1 package (6 ounces) semi-sweet chocolate morsels
- ¼ cup butter
- ½ cup evaporated milk
- 1 jar (7½ ounces) marshmallow cream

Prepare cupcakes as directed on package. Cool. Melt semi-sweet chocolate morsels and butter over hot (not boiling) water; blend well. Remove from heat. Gradually add evaporated milk, stirring until smooth. Let cool to room temperature. Add marshmallow cream and beat until smooth. If desired, vary filling by adding nuts or coconut. Yields frosting for 24 medium cupcakes.

Apple Chip Drop Cookies

Pineapple Party Angel

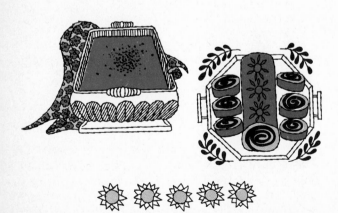

SCOTCH FUDGE

2 packages (6 ounces each) butterscotch flavored
  morsels
1 jar (12 ounces) peanut butter
1 can (14 ounces) sweetened condensed milk

Combine butterscotch morsels and peanut butter
in top of double boiler. Place over hot (not
boiling) water; stir until butterscotch melts and
mixture is smooth. Remove from water. Add
sweetened condensed milk; stir until well blended.
Turn into foil-lined 8-inch square pan. Chill until
firm. Cut in 1-inch squares. Store in covered container. Makes about 64 pieces.

Scotch Fudge

PINEAPPLE PARTY ANGEL

1 can (1 pound, 4½ ounces) crushed pineapple
4 teaspoons unflavored gelatin
2 cups whipping cream
2 cups flaked coconut
1 tablespoon green crème de menthe
   Green food coloring
¼ cup chopped maraschino cherries
1 tablespoon brandy
   Red food coloring
   10-inch angel food cake

Drain pineapple, reserving syrup. Sprinkle gelatin over ½ cup pineapple syrup; place over low heat, stirring until dissolved. Combine with crushed pineapple. Whip cream. Fold half of cream and 1 cup coconut into pineapple. Divide pineapple mixture in half; add crème de menthe and few drops green food coloring to one portion and maraschino cherries, brandy and a few drops of red food coloring to other. Split cake into 3 even layers. Place bottom layer on cake plate; spread with green filling. Top with second layer; spread with pink filling. Cover with top layer and swirl remaining whipped cream over top. Sprinkle with remaining coconut. Decorate with pineapple slices and cherries, if desired. Makes 10 to 12 servings.

WINTER PIE

2 cups canned applesuace
½ cup canned whole cranberries
¾ cup canned pumpkin
½ cup sugar
½ teaspoon salt
2 teaspoons cinnamon
1 teaspoon nutmeg
½ teaspoon ground cloves
2 tablespoons flour
3 eggs
   9-inch unbaked pastry shell

Combine applesauce, cranberries, pumpkin. Add sugar, salt, cinnamon, nutmeg, cloves and flour. Beat eggs; add to mixture. Pour into pastry shell. Bake in preheated oven (400°) 45 minutes or until inserted knife comes out clean. Cool. Makes 8 servings.

INDEX

APPETIZERS, DIPS AND RELISHES

Avocado Corn Dip, 12
Camembert Dip, 12
Cranberry Mincemeat Relish, 15
Curry Apple Relish, 14
Easy Cheese Fondue, 12
Filled Popcorn Balls, 7
Flaming Walnut Paté Balls, 10
Ham 'n' Cheese Logs, 7
Horseradish Dip, 9
Hot Fish Hors D'Oeuvres, 9
Instant Hush Puppies, 7
Jiffy Raisin Relish, 15
Kraut Relish, 14
Nutty Chicken Dip, 12
Parmesan Toast Strips, 7
Party Tarts, 7
Pizza Turnovers, 9
Quick Corn Relish, 14
Salmon Fondue, 13
Shrimp Soup Dip, 12
Smoked Salmon Spread, 9
South of the Border Dip, 12
Spicy Hot Twisters, 9
Stuffed Croissants, 10
Sweet and Wild Relish, 14
Two-Bean Relish, 14

APPLES

Apple Cheese Quiche Pie, 113
Apple Chip Drop Cookies, 120
Apple Nut Drops, 112
Apple Orange Cake, 105
Party Apple Creme, 106
Surprise Apple Crisp, 113

BEANS

Chinese Bean Salad, 25
Fiesta Chili, 16
French Style Bean Casserole, 25
Green Bean Casserole Parmesan, 21
Green Beans Orientale, 25
Marinated Bean Salad, 25
North Star Bean Bake, 25
Sweet Waikiki Beans, 21
'Tater Bean Salad, 16

BEEF

Beef Bourguignon à la Marinade, 7
Beef Cubes Gourmet, 70
Beef Scallopine with Mushroom Sauce, 67
Beef Stroganoff, 67
Beefed-Up Beans, 73
Broiled Round Steak, 70
Casserole Con Queso, 71
Corn Medley Casserole, 69
Creamed Chipped Beef, 73
Hunters' Stew, 73
London Broil Flambé, 68
Mexican Bean Casserole, 70
Pantry Paella, 73
Quick Spaghetti Sauce, 65
Sauce-Topped Meat Loaf, 70
Sauerbraten Pot Roast, 69
Short Ribs Oona Loa, 68
Skillet Beef Supreme, 68
Sloppy Josies, 69
Spaghetti with Meatballs, 66
Steak Au Poivre, 69
Steak Diane, 67
Surprise Meatballs, 65
Swedish Meatballs, 65
Teriyaki, 67

BROCCOLI

Broccoli Chiffon, 26
Broccoli Spears, Curried, 26
Broccoli Supreme Soup, 50
Broccoli-Crab Divan, 59

CARROTS

Carrot Tsimmes, 32
Carrot-Applesauce Duo, 32
Minted Carrots-Wax Beans, 32

CASSEROLES

Baked Bean, 73
Con Queso, 71
Corn Medley, 69
Danish Salmon, 58
Florentine, 59
French Style Bean, 25
Green Bean, Parmesan, 21
Jardinière, 72
Macaroni-Salmon Rarebit, 58
Mexican Bean, 70
Ratatouille Shrimp, 55
Veal and Succotash, 74
Veal-Mushroom Buffet, 74

CHICKEN

Barbecued Chicken
    with Sour Cream Sauce, 94
Chicken Marengo, 90
Chicken Roos Combollo, 92
Chicken Soup Amandine, 49
Cranberry Rose Chicken, 94
Curried Rice-Chicken Croquettes, 92
Wild Rice-Chicken Supreme, 94

CORN

Chuck Wagon Creamed Corn, 26
Corn à la Russe, 29
Corn Relish Salad, 29
Corn-Brussels Sprouts Duo, 30
Kernel Corn Bread, 30
Orange Corn Cups, 30

DESSERTS

Apple Cheese Quiche Pie, 113
Apple Chip Drop Cookies, 120
Apple Nut Drops, 112
Apple Orange Cake, 105
Baked Pears with Port, 97
Banana Spice Cake, 106
Blueberry Rice Supreme, 110
Butter Cream Frosting, 109
Chocolate Chip Cake Brownies, 120
Chocolate Chip Petits Fours, 109
Chocolate Glaze, 109
Chocolate Mousse, 118
Chocolate Refrigerator Cake, 120
Chocolate Walnut Sauce, 106
Coffee Peach Frappe, 97
Creamy Chocolate Frosting, 121
Date Nut Bars, 116
Festive Fruit Platter, 97
Flaming Pineapple Rumba, 98
Fresh Orange Custard, 101
Frosted Date Roll-Ups, 116
Frozen Berry Refrigerator Cake, 111
Frozen Berry Sauce, 111
Fruit Stollen, 119
Fruit with Chutney Dip, 97
Fruited Hard Sauce, 114
Fudge Frost 'n' Bake Cake, 107
Golden Brandy Puff, 110
Graham Cracker Crust, 109
Lemon Coconut Whip, 109
Lemon Filling, 105
Lemon-Filled Banana Cupcakes, 119
Maraschino Nut Loaf, 116
Melon-Strawberry Compote, 97
Meringue-Capped Apricot Tartlets, 116

DESERTS *(continued)*

Party Apple Creme, 106
Pineapple Party Angel, 123
Pink Shower Cake, 114
Princess Parfait, 101
Refrigerator Cheese Cake, 109
Rum Duff, 100
Rum Syrup, 114
Saucy-Raspberry Dessert, 103
Scotch Fudge, 122
Shimmering Mint Mold, 106
Strawberry-Cream Crown, 103
Surprise Apple Crisp, 113
Tarte Angelique, 120
Vanilla Frosting, 105
Walnut Delight, 105
Walnut Pear Chocolate Cream, 98
Walnut Raisin Baba, 114

EGG AND CREPES

Artichoke-Pimiento Omelet, 44
Baked Brunch Ramekins, 47
Cherry Crêpes, 47
Chive-Cottage Cheese Omelet, 45
Crabmeat Omelet, 45
Creamy Scrambled Eggs, 44
Flip-Top Deviled Eggs, 42
Minced Clam Omelet, 45
Mushroom Omelet, 45
Mushroom-Tuna Crêpes, 45
Omelet Marinara, 47
Shrimp Sauced Omelet, 42

LAMB

East-West Lamb Stew, 87
Lamb Scallopine, 87
Skillet Chops and Rice, 80
Savory Lamb Hot Pot, 82

MEAT

Apple 'n' Spice Spareribs, 79
Baked Bean Casserole, 73
Barbecued Chicken, 94
Beef Bourguignon à la Marinade, 71
Beef Cubes Gourmet, 70
Beefed-Up Beans, 73
Beef Scallopine, 67
Beef Stroganoff, 67
Braised Pork Chops, 76
Broiled Round Steak, 70
Calypso Kabobs, 72
Casserole Con Queso, 71
Casserole Jardiniere, 72
Chicken Marengo, 90
Chicken Roos Combollo, 92
City Chicken Legs, 76
Corn Medley Casserole, 69
Cranberry Glazed Turkey Roll, 94
Cranberry Rose Chicken, 94
Creamed Chipped Beef, 73
Curried Rice-Chicken Croquettes, 92
East-West Lamb Stew, 87
Hunters' Stew, 73
Lamb Scallopine, 87
London Broil Flambé, 68
Maiki Ham, 82
Mexican Bean Casserole, 70
Mustard Steak Sauce, 69
Orange Nugget Roast Turkey, 94
Oriental Spareribs, 79
Pantry Paella, 73
Pot of Gold Chops, 80
Pork with Cabbage, 79
Quick Spaghetti Sauce, 65
Sauce-Topped Meat Loaf, 70
Saucy Beans and Franks, 75
Sauerbraten Pot Roast, 69
Savory Lamb Hot Pot, 82
Short Ribs Oona Loa, 68
Skillet Beef Supreme, 68
Skillet Chops and Rice, 80
Skillet Supper, 73
Sloppy Josies, 69
Snappy Western Ham Steak, 80
Spaghetti with Meatballs, 66
Steak Au Poivre, 69
Steak Diane, 67
Surprise Meatballs, 65
Swedish Meatballs, 65
Sweetbreads à la Poulette, 90
Teriyaki, 67
Veal and Succotash En Casserole, 74

MEAT *(continued)*

Veal-Mushroom Buffet Casserole, 74
Veal Paprikash, 76
Veal Cutlet Cordon Bleu, 75
Wild Rice-Chicken Supreme, 94

PEAS

Dilled Petits Pois, 40
Pea Soup Provencal, 49
Peas Aux Herbes, 40
Peas Deluxe, 41

PORK

Apple 'n' Spice Spareribs, 79
Braised Pork Chops with Onion, 76
City Chicken Legs, 76
Maiki Ham, 82
Oriental Spareribs, 79
Pork with Cabbage, 79
Pot of Gold Chops, 80
Skillet Chops and Rice, 80
Snappy Western Ham Steak, 80

POTATOES

Cheese Swirled Potatoes, 39
Potato Clouds, 38
Potato Dumplings, 39
Stuffed Baked Potato, 38

RICE

Chive Rice, 39
Confetti Rice, 39
Rice Ring, 23

SEAFOOD

Baked Seafood Salad, 62
Breaded Shrimp
    with Sour Cream Sauce, 54
Broccoli-Crab Divan, 59
Crab à la Parmentière, 62
Creamed Shrimp and Eggs, 52
Curried Quiche, 59
Danish Salmon Casserole, 58
Florentine Casserole, 59
French-Fried Shrimp
    with Tomato-Wine Sauce, 52
Hawaiian Fillet, 60
Lobster-Walnut Salad Cantonese, 62
Macaroni-Salmon Rarebit Casserole, 58
Quick Spaghetti Clam Sauce, 55
Ratatouille Shrimp Casserole, 55
Salmon Nuggets, 56
Salmon Rabbit, 59
Salmon Ring with Brussels Sprouts, 56
Seafood En Coquille, 52
Shrimp Espanola, 53
Shrimp Lasagna, 55
Shrimp-Rice Bake, 52
Tuna-Wild Rice Bake, 54
Wine Broiled Salmon, 56

SOUPS

Broccoli Supreme Soup, 50
Celery-Cabbage Soup, 49
Chicken Soup Amandine, 49
Curried Salmon and Pea Soup, 51
Jellied Tomato
    Consomme Parisienne, 50
Lobster Bisque Enriched, 49
Mushroom Consomme, 49
Pea Soup Provencal, 49
Puree Mongol, 49
Quick Vichyssoise, 49
Red Hot Tureen, 51
Salmon Chowder, 51
Salmon-Mushroom Soup, 49
Tomato Corn Soup, 51
Tomato Noodle Soup, 51
Tomato Soup Smetana, 51

SPINACH

Creamed Spinach, 37
Saucy Spinach Bake, 35
Spinach Au Gratin, 34
Spinach Ring, 37
Spinach Timbales, 35
Spinach with Bacon, 35
Spinach with Whipped Cream, 37
Spinach-Grapefruit Salad, 36
Spinach-Orange Salad Bowl, 34
Spinach-Tomato Rice, 35

TOMATOES

Broiled Parmesan Tomatoes, 33
Tomato Soup Smetana, 51
Tomato Corn Soup, 51
Tomato Noodle Soup, 51

TURKEY

Orange Nugget, Roast, 94
Roll, Cranberry Glazed, 94

VARIETY MEATS

Baked Bean Casserole, 73
Calypso Kabobs, 72
Casserole Jardiniere, 72
Saucy Beans and Franks, 75
Skillet Supper, 73

VEAL

City Chicken Legs, 76
Skillet Chops and Rice, 80
Sweetbreads à la Poulette, 90
Veal and Succotash En Casserole, 74
Veal Cutlet Cordon Bleu, 75
Veal Paprikash, 76
Veal-Mushroom Buffet Casserole, 74

VEGETABLES

Asparagus Salad Romano, 23
Broccoli Chiffon, 26
Broiled Tomatoes Parmesan, 33
Carrot Tsimmes, 32
Carrot-Applesauce Duo, 32
Cauliflower Pane, 32
Cauliflower with Cheese Sauce, 32
Cheese-Swirled Potatoes, 39
Chinese Bean Salad, 25
Chive Rice, 39
Chuck Wagon Creamed Corn, 26
Confetti Rice, 39
Corn à la Russe, 29
Corn Relish Salad, 29
Corn-Brussels Sprouts Duo, 30
Creamed Spinach, 37
Curried Broccoli Spears, 26
Dilled Petits Pois, 40
Eggplant Parmigiana, 31
Fiesta Chili, 16
French Style Bean Casserole, 25
Garden Medley Salad, 40
Golden Yams, 32
Green Bean Casserole Parmesan, 21
Green Beans Orientale, 25
Kernel Corn Bread, 30
Marinated Bean Salad, 25
Minted Carrots-Wax Beans, 32
Orange-Corn Cups, 31
Orleans Style Corn, 30
North Star Bean Bake, 25
Peas Aux Herbes, 40
Peas Deluxe, 41
Polka Dot Peppers, 16
Potato Clouds, 38
Potato Dumplings, 39
Rice Ring, 23
Roquefort Dressing, 40
Saucy Spinach Bake, 35
Sauerkraut Slaw Alsatian, 38
Scalloped Onions and Almonds, 33
Skillet Red Cabbage, 26
Spinach Au Gratin, 34
Spinach Ring, 37
Spinach Timbales, 35
Spinach with Bacon, 35
Spinach with Whipped Cream, 37
Spinach-Grapefruit Salad, 36
Spinach-Orange Salad Bowl, 34
Spinach-Tomato Rice, 35
Stuffed Baked Potato, 38
Sweet Waikiki Beans, 21
'Tater Bean Salad, 16
Vegetable Bouquet Salad, 40
Zucchini with Lemon Butter Sauce, 39

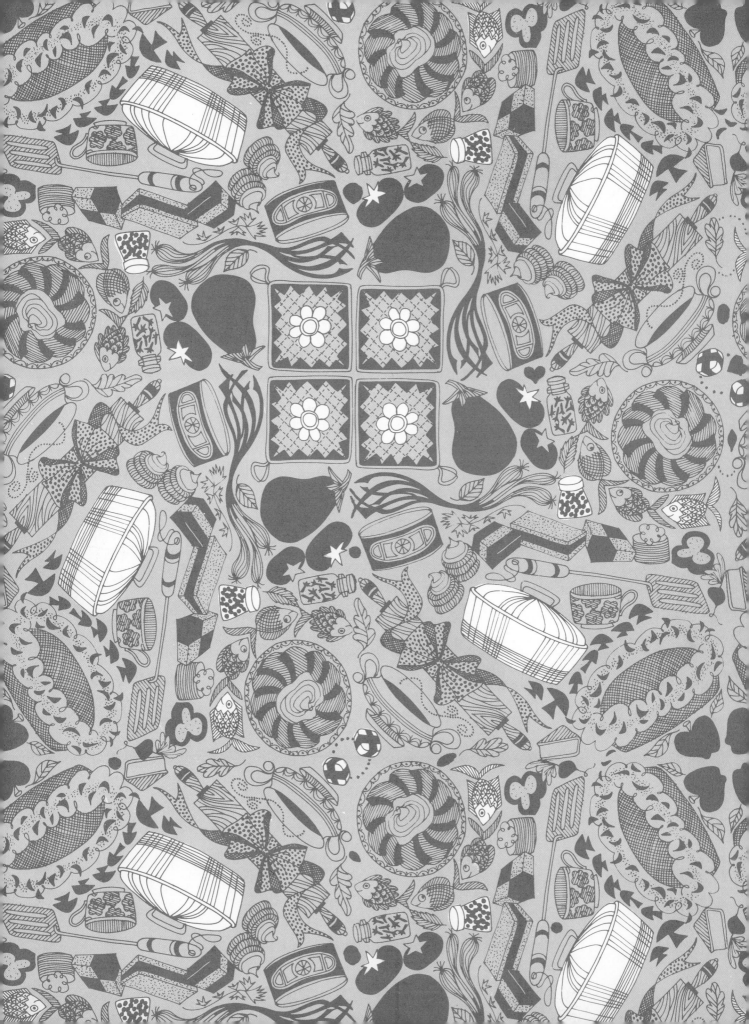